A FATHER'S ADVICE

by Terry King

I0415418

We come into this life alone;

Here to live, to love, to grow.

As we grow, we need to learn;

And pass our knowledge on, you know.

Note: This book is not designed to be read all at once. It certainly wasn't written that way. I had a series of thoughts on various subjects, then organized and edited them. You might wish to treat it like a book of quotations, and simply look under the general category when you wish to hear my thoughts on a particular matter.

However, if you wish to go to sleep, I would recommend that you try to read this book all the way thru at one sitting. I suspect that you will manage to fall asleep within 20 pages or so at most. After all, it is an old and effective technique in defending against boring lectures (if you can manage it without getting caught, that is).

I wrote this book so that I may give you advice on various situations that you are likely to encounter throughout life. I am not trying to tell you what to do. I am simply trying to give you the benefit of what I have observed and often painfully learned over the years. Please pardon my awkward way of saying things.

You are becoming an adult. It is time for you to make your own decisions. I am simply trying to give you some advice. It is up to you as to whether you take it or not.

I do not have much tact. Actually, I have about as much tact as that of a pissed off moose in a china shop. Quite often it seems like my children and I get along together about as well as the moose and the owner of that china shop.

A Father's Advice

By Terry King

I am not a genius. I am not even close to one. But still, I care about you! I am trying to pass on what little wisdom and learning about the world that I have learned. I hope that you will be able to learn something, and thus avoid some of the mistakes that I have made, and those that I have observed other people making. If I manage, through this book, to help prevent you from making one serious mistake in your life, then the labor of writing it will have been worthwhile to me.

I am no angel, nor a perfect being. I absolutely guarantee that I have a lot of faults. I am quite certain that you have noticed quite a few of your parent's faults. I would like you to copy people's virtues, not their faults. If you manage to do this with all the people around you; you will be a much better person.

We all make mistakes in our lives. Do not be afraid to admit to having made a mistake. If you do not admit to making that mistake, you will be making another and more serious mistake.

There is nothing wrong with making mistakes. This is how we learn. The trick is to learn how to avoid making serious ones, preferably before we make them. One way that you can do this is to observe other's mistakes and learn from their bad moves. Another way is to learn from elders that you consider wise. They have a whole lot more experience than you do, hence they have seen a lot more mistakes made than you possibly could have seen yet.

If you have made a mistake that harmed another person, do your best to correct it. Apologize to that person, and make amends for your error as best you can.

I do not care how many or how few things that you own; take care of them. Keep them clean and in good repair, as much as you are able to. The better that you take care of them, the longer that they will last, and the better that they will serve you.

Nothing ever stays the same forever. Change is part of life, get used to it.

I know that it is hard, but learn to be patient. Worthwhile things almost always take time to accomplish. Think about it. How long did it take you to learn to talk, for example?

Don't get so caught up in the day to day grind that you fail to take advantage of the opportunities offered by the area around you. No matter where you are living, there is always something available for you to do or see.

A Paycheck

A paycheck is
A magical thing;
As welcome as
The first sign of spring.
It melts away
Like the first frost,
Leaving you wondering
Where was it lost.
You work so hard
To get that thing;
Where did it go
Was it on a spring?

Plan what to do with your paycheck, don't just spend it. Allow yourself some money just to spend as you wish, but plan the rest. Otherwise, you will swiftly get into trouble.

When you are planning a budget, estimate what your bills will be and then add twenty percent. That way if you have underestimated, forgotten something, or something goes wrong, as usually happens, you have some money available to take care of it. If it turns out that you were correct, then put that extra money in your reserve fund.

Incoming Bills

Bills are coming,
This you know.
Sometimes the amount
Will surprise you, though.
If you cannot
Pay them off,
Your services
Might shut off.
So plan ahead
To avoid this fate;
Or else, your payment
Will be late.

Never go to the bar to cash your paycheck when you have bills to pay out of that paycheck. You are almost inevitably going to have a couple of drinks while you are there. If you recall correctly, alcohol lowers your inhibitions, and you are liable to have a good time there.

The next thing you know, you will wake up in the morning with half of your paycheck gone and not a single bill paid. It is a far wiser idea to go cash your check, pay your bills, and THEN go to the bar to enjoy yourself.

Do not depend on your overtime pay to help keep the bills paid. Plan your budget around your regular paycheck, not the ones with overtime. I know that it sometimes seems like you will always have overtime in some jobs, but sooner or later that overtime is going stop, at least temporarily. If you have been depending on overtime pay, you are going to be hurting when your company starts cutting back on overtime.

Use that overtime pay to catch your past bills up and build up your reserve fund. After that, then use a bit of it for luxuries like eating out once in a while and such.

Do not live up to your income level. Live below it, for example, if you make thirty thousand a year, live at the twenty five thousand a year level. I know that this is very hard to do, especially when you aren't making a whole lot to begin with. At times, it is nearly impossible to do.

Make sure that you pay your bills on time every month. I know that this is difficult, sometimes nearly impossible. If you can't pay all of the bill; at least, pay something on it. This way your creditors will know that you are at least attempting to pay them. This will help your credit rating, and may even improve it.

If you run into trouble paying your bills, let your creditors know as soon as possible. Usually they will attempt to work with you. A word of warning, however; each of those creditors will feel that they are the most important one to be paid first. Make sure that you set the priorities on who gets paid how much, how soon, not them.

It will pay you to purchase a phone card and use it for all your long distance calls, instead of using your long distance service. If you do it this way, you can be certain that your phone bill will not be more than you can afford. It is extremely easy to run up a large long distance phone bill without realizing it.

I know that it is very tempting to write a check just before you get your paycheck, figuring that you will drop your check in the bank in time to cover it. Do not do it. Any number of things could happen to prevent you from doing as you planned. Your car could break down, you could get into an accident and be taken to the hospital, or your paycheck might not arrive on the day that you plan. These are just a few examples of what can happen; and if they do, you are in a worse situation than you started out in.

Normally, they do not happen, but sooner or later they will and then you will be in a mess. Why risk it?

If your money is low and it comes down to a choice between paying a friend back the money he or she loaned you and paying an institution the money due them, pay your friend. You can repair your credit much easier than you can repair your friendships.

If someone calls you, attempting to collect on a debt that you owe them, do not ever agree to send them a postdated check. There is a very good chance that they will attempt to cash it immediately. After all, they are trying to get paid and they would much rather have it sooner than later. Send them the check when you have the money in the bank and not a moment before.

If you have gotten yourself into financial trouble, it is time to stop and think. Quit panicking, it will not help you one little bit. Start assessing what you actually need, not just what you want to have. This is not a time to think about impressing people; it is a time to think about what you actually need to survive.

You do need a place to stay, but it does not necessarily have to be a fancy place. Your ancestors managed to live in log cabins and sod houses that they built themselves, you can do the same if necessary.

You do need clothes, but you most likely have quite a few of them already. It is not absolutely necessary to buy brand new clothes. Many a person gets their clothes from thrift shops, and manages to look quite well. You can do the same.

You do need transportation, but it does not necessarily have to be a fancy new car. What you need is something to get you where you are going safely, reliably, and inexpensively. Consider selling the car you have and getting a less expensive one. Many a person has gotten along quite fine with an old junker until they could afford something better.

Instead of going out to eat for lunch, why not pack a lunch for work. It will not kill you not to eat at a fast food joint every day. You do not have to eat as fancy as you have been doing. Quit buying all those prepared meals and start buying the basic ingredients and make them yourself. When you peel your potatoes, don't throw away the peelings. Save them in water, and fry them up for breakfast.

If you look around at what you have been doing, you will find a lot of ways to save on expenses. Then you can use those savings to get yourself caught up on your bills. Pennies and dimes do add up, you know.

In Trouble

If your paycheck
Is so small,
That you can't
Pay bills at all;
Find a way
To increase your pay.
Do not spend it all
On play.
Cut your bills
At least in half,
And be picky
About which half.
You do not need
To go to malls;
Or even eat
Fast food, at all.
Right now,
You must be cheap;
Otherwise,
You'll get in deep.

When someone calls you and says that they are trying to save you money, they are generally attempting to get you to do business with them rather than with the company that you are currently doing business with.

From time to time, you will most probably receive offers in the mail trying to sell you so many books, videos, or music albums for the price of one, if you will join a club. Of course, once you become a member of this club, they will send you a list of their products to choose from, and their main selection will usually be sent to you automatically unless you decline it within a specified time.

To my mind, the catch is that the company is gambling that you will not get around to declining it in time and you will shortly accumulate a debt to this company for that product. I do not advise you to accept this type of offer, but if you do, make sure that you keep up with it. Get the products that you want and cancel your membership as soon as possible. This, in my opinion, is the best way to stay out of trouble, if you decide to accept their offer.

Whenever you encounter someone who is trying to sell you something, and they tell you that the competing product or service is lousy; alarm bells should be going off in your head. It is a very good possibility that the product that they are trying to sell you is equally bad or worse; so be very wary.

Bills

Bills are like weeds.
You know it's true.

If you've too many,
They'll make you blue.
So knock them down,
And do it quick;
Else your paycheck
Will sink like a brick.

Cell Phones:

Cell phones were not very common, when I
originally wrote this book. Now, they are
everywhere, and almost everyone has one. They
are needed, in today's world, in a lot of ways.
However, there are definitely things that you
should consider, when using them.

It is dangerous for you to be using them, as you
are walking down the street. First off, it shows
onlookers that you are distracted, and not paying
attention. If a thief is watching you, you have just
become a possible target for them, especially if
your cell phone looks to be an expensive one.

Driving while using them is very dangerous,
ESPECIALLY if you are texting. Laws are
starting to spring up, about this, and rightfully so,
in my opinion. A lot of people have gotten into
accidents because one of the drivers was using
their phone. I have nearly been killed, on several
occasions, while flagging for road construction,
by drivers using their phones. PLEASE do not do
this!

It's a good idea to have a portable battery for your phone. It helps, when you are running low on power. I rather like having a portable battery that can charge either by sunlight or electricity. This can help enormously, if you are in a situation where there is an extended power outage.

I find it helps to have a spare, pay as you go phone, available, with all your contacts on it. This way, if something happens to your main phone, you have a backup phone available for immediate use.

Choices

Attitude is very important. You will get a whole lot more accomplished, a whole lot easier, if you have a positive attitude rather than a negative one.

Make sure that you help in the common chores around your home. You often ask your parents for their help in accomplishing things that you wish to do. Why should they help you, if you do not help them? The dishes have to be washed, the home has to be kept clean, the garbage must be disposed of, why shouldn't you do your fair share of these things?

Have a plan for what you want to accomplish in your life, don't just drift through high school and life. You will undoubtedly change your plan from time to time, but always have some sort of plan of what you want to be doing in, say, five or ten years from now. Then work towards your plan.

Always work towards the long term benefits as opposed to the short term. The short term is more attractive, but the long term pays one heck of a lot better.

There is a perfect example of this in financial planning. If you save a small amount of money each week, from your paycheck, for your retirement from the time that you are eighteen and do not <u>ever</u> touch it, you will tend to have a very comfortable retirement fund. Compound interest works wonders over a long term period. Do the math yourself. You will see what I am talking about.

After a while, you will be able to change it into a higher interest account. Move the whole amount, and ensure that you can continue to make small deposits into it. This way, you will be able to take advantage of the compound interest on the whole amount. Otherwise, you will be starting from scratch, with the money in the lower interest bearing account, and not being able to take advantage of the effects of compound interest on the whole amount.

I have found that this is true generally throughout life. If you strive for the long term benefits rather than going after your short term opportunities, you will be much better off and you will have fewer troubles in your life.

Always have a backup plan in case something goes wrong.

Make your living honestly. You may make less money, but you will sleep better at night and you will not have to worry about being caught.

If you are not willing to have what you are doing known, then you probably shouldn't be doing it in the first place.

There are going to be times when you have to choose between several alternatives, all bad. Some of them are going to be worse than the other possibilities, so chose carefully.

Do things the legal way. It will save you a lot of aggravation, worry, and money in the long run.

There will be times in your life when you are going to be so upset that you are not going to care what you do, one way or the other. Be careful, this is a very dangerous time for you. You are liable to act in an extremely stupid fashion, so think very carefully before you make any decisions.

If possible, postpone any important decisions until you are in a better mood.

Sooner or later, you are going to regret some of your past actions. Often these are major decisions that you have made. This happens to everyone. I know that it is hard, but try not to dwell on them. Learn from what has happened and move on with your life.

Remember, you are not God, and you do not know everything. If you made the best and fairest decision that you possibly could, using all the information that you had available to you at the time; then you are doing the best that you can.

I do not expect you to be perfect, so do not expect yourself to be perfect. If you do expect perfection out of yourself, you are going to be needlessly upset, a lot of times. Instead, analyze what went wrong, and how you can do things better next time.

We do not know what the long term cffccts of our actions are. Remember the old poem:

> For want of a nail,
> A shoe was lost.
> For want of a shoe,
> A horse was lost.
> For want of a horse,
> A rider was lost.
> For want of a rider,

A battle was lost.
For want of a battle,
A kingdom was lost;
And all for the want
Of a horseshoe nail.

Therefore, you should always do your best. One little action of yours may have a profound effect on the life of someone you have never met halfway across the world.

We never know just how long our lives will be. Just deciding on the spur of the moment to go down to the corner store may be what ends your life. Therefore, live each day as though it is the last day that you may have on this earth.

If you are unhappy with your life the way it is, think about why you are unhappy. Carefully analyze what it is about your life that makes you unhappy. Then, figure out how to solve the problem or problems.

You might end up moving far away and starting all over again. This happens to a lot of people, so don't feel that you are the only one. Hang in there, starting all over again is always rough.

Choices

Little do we know

What cost we'll pay,
For each choice
That we make.
We walk into the future,
Far blinder than a bat.
Yet somehow, we're expected
To make it come out right.
A chance misstep,
A spoken word,
And life's
All gone away.
So let this
Be your watchword,
While you still
Have choice.
A cheering word,
A helping hand;
Will help things
Come out right.

Cooking

It will pay you to learn how to cook. I, myself,
was forced to learn how to cook breakfasts in
sheer self interest. After my brothers and I had
reached a certain age, my mother refused to cook
us breakfast anymore. If we wanted to eat
anything before we went to school, we had to fix
it ourselves.

She was willing to teach us how to cook it, but
it was up to us if we wanted to learn or not. If we
didn't want to learn, it was perfectly all right with
her if we ate cold cereal for the rest of our lives.

I didn't learn how to cook dinners until I started living in my own place. For quite a while I existed on hamburger helper type meals, instant potatoes, and canned vegetables. Finally, I broke down and asked my mother for a cookbook for Christmas. Try not to let this happen to you. Learn to cook before you move out on your own. You will eat a lot better; and cooking your meals is a lot less expensive than going out to eat all the time.

It will save you a lot of embarrassment if you learn how to cook something before you try to cook it for someone else. One person I knew attempted to bake pies for a holiday dinner once. It was the first time that she had ever attempted to make a pie. She had bought ready-made crusts from the store and used those. Unfortunately, she hadn't known to take the wax paper out from in between the shells. We discovered her error when we started to eat the pies. Her husband and I were extremely amused, but she was highly embarrassed.

Cleaning

Keep your place clean. You never know when you might have a visitor whom you wish to impress. Even if the place that you are living in is a dump, keep your part of it clean. That way, your visitor will think that: "Hey, this person may not have much money, but at least they are clean."

Otherwise they will think that you have about what you deserve in the way of living quarters and salary, and you will lose a lot of respect in their eyes.

Your home does not have to be spotless. It should, however, look like an adult human being lives there, not a herd of five year old children.

Dealing With Other People

> Mind your own business
> Is a good rule.
> It helps keep you
> From acting a fool.
> If you choose
> Your mouth to shoot;
> You may get
> A punch in the snoot.

Respect other people's beliefs, even though you disagree with them. They have the absolute right to believe as they please, just as you do.

Have consideration for the rights of other people. This will save you from having a whole lot of trouble.

Do not put up with racial, sexual, or religious discrimination. It is just plain wrong. Simply because someone is of a different race, sex, or religion than you are does not mean that they are not a good person. It also does not mean that they cannot do the job for which they are applying. They may have different ways than you do, but that does not mean that their ways are wrong, just different.

Do not make the mistake of thinking that your lifestyle, sexual orientation, or religion is the only right way to live. It is not; it is simply the way that you happen to live.

A person's race, and their sexual orientation are not of their choosing. It is just the way that they are. Do not dislike or harass them simply because of those things. It does not make them any better or worse than you are, merely different.

It is highly unlikely that you will ever be in a position to "save the world". However you can, every day, help make your part of it a little bit better. Look around you, there is always an opportunity to help make your community a bit better for those who live in it.

Change

We cannot change
The whole world wide.
But we can affect
Those by our side,
By our choices
And our caring.

Show some love
And do some sharing.
You can help
Change someone's hell,
Into a better
Place to dwell.

Do not fail to help others as you go thru life. It will come back to you at some unexpected time.

Be kind to the elderly and handicapped people. Help them where you can. You might well be in their shoes one day.

Do not worry too much about what other people think about you. There is always going to be someone who does not like who you are or what you are doing. What you have to worry about is what you think of yourself.

Respect other people's rights to do as they please. You may give them advice, but what they decide to do is up to them. It is their life, not yours.

It is not up to you to make the other person do right. That is their decision. You just worry about whether what you are doing is right or not. That is a big enough job for you.

With machinery, moving parts require lubrication to keep them running smoothly and to prevent excessive wear and tear. This lubrication is generally a petroleum based product or something similar. With people, the lubrication is politeness. Always be polite, especially if you do not like that person.

Be considerate of other people's feelings.

Always try to give the other person the benefit of the doubt, especially when he or she is being really rude. After all, they may just be having a really bad day.

Try hard not to take your bad mood out on others. You will get along with people a lot better.

When you know someone is hurting, do not bother them. Above all, do not deliberately try to piss them off; because if you do, they are liable to clobber you, suddenly, severely, and without warning. Do not look to me for sympathy at that point, as I will tell you that it was your own fault.

Do not ever be certain that your way is the only right way to do something. A technique that works well for you may well not work at all for someone else. Everyone is different, so everyone finds different ways to do things.

Techniques

Everyone has
Their own style,
And ways of
Doing things.
"To each their own"
Is a good way
Of looking at
This kind of thing.
Treat everyone
With respect,
And know
They might be right.
Who knows,
It just might be,
That you both
Are in the right.

When you are arguing with someone over an issue, always remember that you might be wrong too, even though you are convinced that they are wrong. It is also a possibility that you might both be partially correct. Heck, you might both be completely wrong, too.

When you are trying to convince someone that they are wrong, make your arguments and then give them time to think about it. I do not mean two minutes, either. It takes time for someone to look at what they are saying or doing, and decide that they are wrong. For example, how long does it take you to admit that you are wrong, especially when you are mad?

Do not expect other people to be perfect. Everyone makes mistakes. As long as they are making an honest effort to do their best, be tolerant of any mistakes that they might make.

Very few people like being made to look foolish or ridiculous in front of people. If you do that to them, you have most probably made them into an enemy, so try hard not to put them in that position.

When judging another person's actions that happened in an emergency situation, kindly remember that you were not there at the time. You have all the time in the world to make your decision; but they had perhaps thirty seconds, if they were lucky, to make that decision. You do not have fear as a companion in making your judgment. They undoubtedly did, and fear is not helpful in making good decisions.

Do not be afraid to show your love for another person, no matter who they are or where you are.

Cherish love where ever you find it.

Do your best to be tolerant of teenagers. You were one recently, and yes, you were just as mouthy and certain that you knew everything; and that everyone, that was much older than you, didn't know a single thing.

If you want to find out what a person is like, look at the small things around them, especially when they do not know that you are around. Watch the effect that they have on the people around them.

If animals do not like a person whom you happen to know, beware. Something is quite probably wrong with that person. Remember, animals tend to see into a person's essential character more than people do. If they do not like him or her, there is a reason for it. It would behoove you to find out that reason before you decide to trust that person.

Make sure that you listen to your elders and give them respect. Remember, they have a whole lot more experience in dealing with people than you do. There are going to be a lot of times when you are coming up to something new to you, but they have been thru it or known people who have been thru it. They will be able to give you valuable advice if you are wise enough to seek their counsel.

You cannot ever make someone happy for the rest of their life. You can cheer them up from time to time, but in the end, whether they are happy or not is up to them. It is their attitude that is the determining factor. We all face disappointments in life. How a person deals with them is what matters most.

Never steal from your family or screw them over. Do right by them and they are likely to be there for you when you need help. If you screw them over, it is unlikely that they will help you when you need it.

Measure the caliber of your friends. If they are always getting you in trouble, are they truly your friends? Do they try to keep you out of trouble? If you are in trouble, do they try to help you?

Be loyal to your family and friends. If you think that they are wrong in something, take them aside and talk to them privately about it. Do not tell them that they are wrong in front of the whole world.

If a couple of your friends start fighting and you don't want to take either side; don't sit on the fence in between them. You are liable to get hit with the mud that they are throwing. Sit down a bit further away from the fight.

Do remember that not everyone notices hints. Some people are simply oblivious to them. It is not that they are stupid, it is just the way that they are. With that type of person, you simply have to tell them what it is that you are trying to tell them rather than giving them hints. It is either that or you will get very frustrated with them, and it is not their fault. That is just the way that they are.

There is nothing wrong with practical jokes. However, first of all, make sure that that person will appreciate it. Secondly, <u>always</u> make sure that no one can get hurt. If there is even the slightest possibility that someone could, don't pull the joke. It is not worth it.

There is always going to be someone around willing to help you spend your hard-earned money on foolish things. Don't let them do it.

Occasionally you may overhear part of a conversation and hear someone say something that sounds really wrong. Before you start assuming that what they said was terrible, why don't you find out what the whole conversation was about. Quite often, once you find out about the whole conversation, you will see that that person had not really said anything wrong after all.

This sort of thing happens quite frequently, so do not jump before you know the whole story.

First impressions are important, there is no denying that. They can be countered, but it will take time to do so. Quite often, as in a job interview, you will not have that time. Therefore, take the time to make a good first impression.

Be yourself. Do not try to impress someone by being someone that you are not or claiming skills that you do not have. You may impress them, but sooner or later, they are going to find out the truth. Then how will you look to them?

Especially when you are angry, stop and think before you say or do anything. Otherwise, you are very liable to regret your actions.

There are an awful lot of people around who love to cause trouble for other people, especially for those that they dislike. One of the ways that they love to do this is to wait until you are already annoyed and then deliberately annoy you further. They are betting that they can say or do something to get you even madder; and that then you will say or do something that gets you into trouble. Don't give them that satisfaction.

Death

Death is a part of the cycle of life. It is inevitable for all of us. You might get out of paying taxes, but sooner or later death will tap you on your shoulder. It will come to everyone that you know, sooner or later. When someone that you love dies, it is very normal to miss them. It hurts very badly.

It is ok to be sad that the time that you spent with them was so short, and that you wish that it had been much longer. Be glad though, that you did get to spend time with them. Remember the good times that you had with them and the lessons that they taught you.

Veil of Tears

They've walked this path
Before me;
Thru the Veil of Tears.
I feel their strength
Around me;
Allaying my fears.
Unseen hands
Surround me;
Holding me upright.
They're here to help me
Make it through
This long and endless night.
Each of us
Must make
This journey in our life.
Walk this path
While honoring
What they've done in life.

Distractions

If you start necking while you are cooking, you are liable to burn your dinner.

Distractions abound in this world of ours. Do not let yourself be distracted from doing what you have to do. Not paying attention to what you are doing is one of the major causes of accidents.

Divorce

Divorce is a serious matter. Do not undertake it lightly.

No matter how mad that you are at your former partner, do your best to be fair with him or her. Do not attempt to screw them over in the divorce settlement.

Do not use the children that you have had together as weapons to hurt your former partner.

Make it clear to your children that they are not the cause for your divorce. It is not their fault, it is yours and your former partner's.

If you have gotten a divorce, and have found yourself completely unable to pay the child support that you are required to pay, even with a drastic reduction in your expenses; there is a possible solution. It is, however, a drastic solution. Think it through very carefully, and with all due care for the ramifications; before you terminate your parental rights.

Remember, if you ask this of the courts, your child is going to be aware of this, and it will affect your relationship with him/her for the rest of your lives. If you are successful in your request, you will no longer have any right to know anything about him/her, and no say in their affairs. It is a very serious step. Do not undertake it lightly.

Do not make it hard for your former partner to see your children.

Make the time to see your children as often as possible. You are still their parent, and they are still your responsibility.

Remember, after the divorce, your former partner still has a say in how those children should be raised. They are still his or hers children.

Especially after a divorce, children tend to try to play one parent off against the other. Don't let it happen.

After the divorce, as time goes by, both you and your former partner may acquire new mates. They will each have opinions on how those children should be raised. Your new partner's opinion should be given the same amount of consideration as your former spouse's new partner's opinion. It is only fair.

Memories

I loved you once;
And still I remember

The taste of
Your lips on mine,
The way you felt
When you leaned on me,
When you needed someone near.

Our love dissolved
In fiery tears.
We hurt each other
At the end,
When once you were so dear.
Where was the fault?
'Twas both of course.

A need you had
That I didn't fill.
A quarrel we had,
And pride forbade
"I'm Sorry".
But still I remember
The love that once we had.

Dreams

There is absolutely nothing wrong with daydreaming, in its proper time and place. It helps us define what we want to do and be. However, if you do it when you are supposed to be concentrating on something else, like school or work, it tends to get you in trouble.

Do not fail to work to turn your dreams into reality. If you do not, they most likely will not happen and you will not deserve them if they do.

Hope is the one thing that we can always have. To turn your hopes and dreams into reality takes work and dedication.

<u>Drugs</u>

A very good rule to follow is never to use any type of drugs or alcohol when you are on an emotional high or low. Either way, if you do so, you are opening the door to addiction.

If you use them when you are on an emotional low and you start feeling better, you will then tend to use it to escape any time that you feel depressed. On an emotional high, you will tend to associate that elation with being high and attempt to recreate that feeling by using the drug again.

If someone tells you that alcohol is not a drug, they are full of baloney. It is just as much a drug as marijuana or cocaine. It just happens to be a more socially acceptable drug, that is all.

Do not ever allow someone to talk you into taking any type of drink or drug that you do not wish to. They are not doing you any favors.

One of the problems that I have noticed about alcohol is that people tend to be more aggressive and argumentative then they are normally. This has led to a lot of people being injured and/or killed.

I have never noticed this about the use of marijuana. In fact, from what I have seen, people tend to be more mellowed out than aggressive. However, I am not a scientist and have not studied this extensively.

In any case, you should not drive while you are under the influence of any drug as your reaction speed is lowered and your judgment is impaired. You are risking the lives and health of yourself, your passengers, and people that you do not even know.

Alcohol (or drugs) and weapons do not mix well. Many a person is in prison who has tried to mix them. Do not let yourself become one of those people.

Too many friends

Have gone down a path,

That I,

I cannot follow.

The price is high

To go down that path,

Although,

There is some pleasure.

Forgetfulness

Is a gain,

But it never

Lasts too long.

The loss of all

That one holds dear,

Is the price,

That you may pay.

<u>Education</u>

Getting an education is very important. Otherwise, you only tend to qualify for low paying jobs and that makes for a hard life.

In this world, you have to develop a skill or provide a service that people are willing to pay for in order to make a living. School is often a very important tool in developing that skill. To provide a service, you have to know what people want and are willing to pay for. For that, you need information on how the world works and what people are likely to need in the future.

<u>Quitting School</u>

If you quit
Formal school,
You might well
Be acting a fool.
Without training,
Jobs pay so small;
You hardly see
Your paycheck
At all.
No money for fun,
Not even to date;
Try to avoid
That terrible fate.

If you are weak in an area of learning, study that area the hardest of all. I knew one person that was not very good in the area of English in his high school years. He knew that he had to improve if he wished to go to college, so he studied that area the hardest of all. He ended up making English his major in college.

Study mathematics, especially statistics and probability theory. It is essential for understanding any field of science. In addition to that, probability theory will be useful throughout your life, especially if you decide to gamble.

It will pay you to study history, not only the political type that the schools tend to favor, but the social history of various times as well. If nothing else, it will convince you that however rough that you have it right now; your ancestors have survived much worse situations than you are in. Therefore, you can also survive whatever situation that you are presently in.

One good way to study social history is to read novels based in a particular era, written by an author that has done their research, and has a reputation for historical accuracy. They will be able to give you some sense of the way people lived back then, while telling you a very good tale.

Three particular authors come to my mind for this sort of thing. They are: F. Van Wyck Mason, Jean M. Auel, and John Jakes. I am quite sure that there are many others. There is one minor drawback with books by these authors; their books are quite long. It will take you more than one evening to read them. The books are extremely good though, and well worth the reading.

Try to make sure that you have some kind of training in a career by the time that you finish school. This will make it much easier to find a good paying job that will enable you to have a place of your own instead of having to live with your parents.

If you only have a high school education, it is going to be harder for you to find a good job. You will likely have to develop some skills in order to get a good paying job. This takes time, so don't get discouraged. Learn from each job that you are on, they all can teach you valuable lessons.

If you can't afford to go to college, go to the library and read. Don't bother too much with the fiction section; read the nonfiction books. You can also use intralibrary loans to get books about a subject that you are interested in. This will improve your education.

There are all sorts of magazines available for you to read as well, many of which are devoted to a specific field of interest. If you wish to learn about something that you are interested in, read that particular type of magazine and as many back issues of it that you can get your hands on. You will be surprised just how much that you can learn about it from them. This is another way to improve your education.

Buy a book of quotations and read it. There generally is a lot of wisdom in them that you can apply to everyday life.

Go visit a museum from time to time. It will broaden your mind and often relax you.

Read some philosophy occasionally, and think about what that person is trying to say.

Overconfidence does not pay off. It is very easy to become overconfident in a skill that you have recently acquired. Be very wary of that. If you don't, you are heading for trouble.

Never stop learning. There is always something new to learn, and learning will always pay off in the long run.

Envy

There are going to be times in your life when it seems like everyone has more money than you do. You are sitting there without a penny in your pocket to spend, and everyone around you is eating and drinking and having a good old time.

At times like this, it is a good idea to look at what you do have and think about how your situation could be worse. There is always someone who is much worse off than you are, even though you feel like you have absolutely nothing.

There is always going to be someone that has more of something (like looks, talent, money, etc.) than you do, so why waste the time and energy bemoaning your fate? Use that time and energy on doing something worthwhile instead. Concentrate on improving what you do have. If nothing else, do some drawing, read a book, something, anything to keep from wasting your energy on useless envy.

If you are envious of someone that has more talent than you do, consider the fact that all the talent in the world is useless if that person doesn't try to develop that talent. A person with modest talent who persistently works hard to develop that talent; in the long run, does better then someone with a lot of talent who doesn't work at it.

Experts

There are going to be many times in your life that you are going to deal with experts in a field that you are either slightly familiar with or not familiar with at all. Do remember that they are the experts, not you, and listen to their advice. You do not have to take it, but be sure that you have a very good reason to go against their advice.

Experts have been wrong before, and quite often, spectacularly so. By and large, though, they know what has been done in their field and what is possible to do, given the limits of the technology available.

For example, look at flying. The experts all said that it couldn't be done. It was done, eventually; however technology had to improve tremendously before it could be accomplished. How many thousands of times have people attempted it before flight became possible?

There are dishonest people in every profession, so be wary. Always get a second opinion before you commit large amounts of money.

Finances

It is better to have no credit than bad credit. If you borrow money, make sure that you repay it on time every month.

Before you borrow money, consider carefully all of the ways that things can go wrong, and have a plan to take care of them. What happens if you get laid off or sick? Will you still be able to repay the money that you borrowed? You should always have a backup plan in case things go wrong.

Always have a reserve fund. I can guarantee you that it will pay off to do so. You never know when something can happen that will require money to solve the problem. This is why the experts recommend having a month's pay in the bank at all times. They are right.

<u>Saving Money</u>

Save some money
From each pay;
I guarantee
You'll need it someday.
It's so easy
To spend it now,
But what if
Life goes: "Pow!"?
Your job is gone,
Or your car may die;
Without reserves
You'll want to cry.
So take my advice,
And stash some cash.
Someday you'll need it
In a flash.

Whenever you get a large chunk of money coming into your life (for example: an income tax refund) that you are not accustomed to dealing with, STOP. Put it in the bank, except for perhaps five percent of it. You are going to want to celebrate and you are going to spend some of it foolishly, so allow yourself a small amount to enjoy. Then, after you have it out of your system; think very carefully about what to do with the rest of it.

Remember what I told you about having a reserve fund? Now is the ideal time to add to or establish that reserve fund. Having a reserve fund will always pay off in the long run.

If that money is still burning a hole in your pocket, stash it away in short term certificates of deposit. This will enable you to have some time to think about how you would like to use it to improve your life, without having the easy access to it that unsettles your thinking.

Having good credit is very important. This enables you to take care of emergencies that you have not planned for and do not have the cash for at the time.

It is sometimes very easy to get credit, especially when you are young and just starting out. Be very careful not to get too many loans. It is quite easy to get in over your head.

Be careful with credit cards. They are very useful and nice to have; but you can get in a lot of trouble with them too. They make it easy to create bills that you will have difficulty in paying.

When you have and use multiple credit cards, it is extremely easy to overestimate your ability to pay them off.

Be very careful that you do not overextend yourself on money matters. It is far better to purchase a used car and have some money and/or credit available for emergencies than to buy a new car and have no spare money.

Before you commit to purchasing a new vehicle, check to see how much your car insurance is going to cost you. With full coverage insurance, the premiums are liable to meet or exceed your car payments. Make certain that you will be able to handle both payments with ease. Remember, the cost of stuff seldom goes down, while your earnings can drop drastically at any time.

Once you have started putting money aside for your retirement, you are going to have to look for ways to make that money grow. It won't be enough just to place it in a savings account, you are will to need to invest it. Obviously, it is going to take a little while before you have enough money saved up to make any investments, but you should do it as soon as you can.

Talk to your bank's investment counselor. They should be able to help you and most likely it will not cost anything. Remember, banks are in the business of handling other people's money, so they have well qualified personnel. If they do not, they go out of business.

If your credit is in a mess, do not apply for any more loans. Look up your credit report and find out exactly how much you owe and who you owe it to. Quite often, if you haven't been paying your past debts, your debtors may have sold your debt to a debt collector. If you are not careful, you may end up paying the wrong person to cancel your debt. Start paying off all those old bills and keep each and every receipt that you get.

After you get everything paid off, check your credit report again. If something is still showing that you owe money, contact the credit bureau and prove to them that you now have that debt paid off.

Wait a year before you even think about trying for any type of loan and pay all your bills on time or even ahead of time. Then, start small and apply for a loan to buy something relatively inexpensive. Make sure that you make each payment on time or even a bit ahead of time. Then, do it again or perhaps try for a secured credit card. Keep doing this and you will rebuild your credit gradually.

Government and the System

The Systems

The systems
We have built,
Are really
Quite amazing.
We've built them up,
One by one;
With money
As a basis.

There's seldom
Any thought,
On building them
To match.
The end result
Is as bright;
As pouring out some gas,

And tossing in a match.

Always study the rules of any system that you are under. Usually, you are told most of the ones that apply to you at the time that you enter that system. It is very seldom that you are told all of the rules. Part of the reason for that is that they do not want to overload you with information that you don't need at the time. It is the same way that it is done when you start a new job. They give you enough information to get you started with, and then you learn more after you get used to doing that stuff. It is a very good idea to study all the rules, not just the ones that you have been told about. It will always pay off in the long run.

With government you usually are expected to learn the rules (laws) by osmosis; at least it seems that way to me. The government very seldom tells you the exact wording of those laws; probably because they are usually worded in a barely comprehensible fashion.

Apparently high government service seems to cause residents thereof to forget how to speak or write in plain, simple language. That is the only reasonable explanation for the phenomena that I have been able to discern. Please let me know if you happen to discover a better explanation.

Wherever you go, there is always a system to get things done. It doesn't matter what your job is or where you are at, there is a system there.

Oftentimes, especially at a job with few employees, it can be rather chaotic. However, the system works for the person or group who owns the company. Work within the system, even if you want to change that system.

This is especially true of government. Whatever government you are under, there are a lot of times when it seems like the system that is in effect really sucks. Hang in there and work within the system to get the problem solved. I <u>know</u> that it seems to take forever and that it doesn't seem that anything will ever get changed.

You have to remember that when a system is established by a large group of people (i.e. a government), there is a lot of inertia keeping it in place. You are only one person, you cannot expect to change the system all by yourself.

Basically, you have to get other people involved in changing the system with you. Even if you are in a position of power within the government, you cannot hope to change the whole system by yourself. There has to be other people who also recognize that there is a problem and agree on a solution to fix that problem.

If you can get thirty or more percent of the people under that government to recognize that there is a problem <u>and</u> agree on a solution, you have a good shot at being able to fix that problem.

Government is established to take care of the common needs of a group of people. It can only exist if that group of people consent to be governed by it. If a large majority of the people do not consent to be governed by it, that government is in severe danger of ceasing to exist.

You are a part of that group of people. You have a right to have a voice in how your government functions, just as you should have a say in the function of any group to which you belong. You also have a duty to make sure that your government functions properly. Therefore, make sure that you exercise your rights to participate in your government as much as you can.

If you have the right to vote, make sure that you do so intelligently and with care for the consequences of your actions. Make sure that you vote for the person that you think will do the job to the best of his or her ability, regardless of their political party.

If you think that you are throwing your vote away by voting for the candidate of a minor political party, you are mistaken. Your vote does count. You are making your voice heard. You are saying that: "Hey, this is the person that I think is best suited for that job."

Just because the majority does not agree with you does not mean that your opinion does not count. Remember, minor political parties become major political parties if enough people vote for them. However, this does not happen if the people do not vote for who they think is the best candidate, but rather who they think has the best chance of winning the election.

What is your political philosophy? What do you think that government should do and what they should not do? How do you think that they should go about doing it? Once you have the answers to these questions, then look at the political parties and candidates in your area and choose who you should vote for.

Never, ever trust the government or the people in office very far. Keep a close eye on them and what they do.

It often appears that no one in high political office has any idea whatsoever, what it is like to bust their arse for a small living. If you ever achieve high office, do not be like that.

Remember, you are supposed to look after the interests of all the people, including the ones who bust their arse for a meager living. There is an awful lot of people in that situation in this world, and they are usually the ones who get screwed over the worst by those in power. I suspect that this is because that those in power feel that those people don't really matter, and that the small people have no power to affect them.

After all, they cannot begin to contribute to any political campaign funds, in any meaningful way, like the big contributors can. Neither can they make any large effects on the economy, like businesses can. Besides, most of the people who are barely making a living seldom vote in the first place, as far as they are concerned. Therefore, they don't matter.

They do come in handy as cannon fodder, once in a while, though.

If and when you are in a position of power, be careful that you do not abuse that power. Remember, power corrupts; and it is extremely easy to make yourself believe that what you want to happen is what should be happening. This is not necessarily the case.

Those people under you have rights, make certain that you do not abuse their rights or those people. You have been placed in a position of trust, do not abuse it.

The laws that you are expected to obey are not always right, but do your best to abide by them. If you feel that they are wrong, do your best to change those laws.

Even if you are under a very corrupt and abusive government, think it through thoroughly; before you engage in violent revolt against it. The price that you pay may be very high indeed, and others besides yourself will also pay the cost, quite often innocent parties.

If you ever start thinking that your government is really bad and must go, no matter what the means, take a good look at history first. If you look closely at the types of governments that have been in existence in the past, and then compare it to your government; it may not look nearly as bad as some of those that have been in existence.

Take a thorough look back into history and the rights that the common people had a few hundred years or so ago. Go back even farther if you would like to. No matter what continent, or portion of history, that you look at; usually you will find that the common people were usually given much less regard and care for than the animal pets of the people in power. Quite often, they were essentially slaves, or nearly so.

You may well live in a society that is unjust, whether towards other people or to a group that you belong to. Remember what I have told you before. Use what political power that you do have to change the situation. Join an organization that is dedicated to peacefully changing that situation.

An unjust society takes time to change. It may well be that it will never fully come to pass in your lifetime. However, continue the struggle. You have to change people's attitudes, not just the laws. That can only be done by persuasion, not laws. It is much easier to change the laws, but it will not completely solve the situation.

Do not despair, it has been done before. The Irish people in the US are a good example. Once upon a time, there was many an employer who had a sign on his door: "No Irish need apply". Now, no employer has that sign on his door and there is very little, if any, prejudice towards the Irish people.

One day you may have to ask for assistance from the government for basic living expenses. Swallow your pride, keep your mouth shut, and do what has to be done. Do not stay on it, though. Get off it as soon as possible and earn your own living.

Whenever you ask for any type of government aid there is a lot of red tape. It takes a lot of time for anything to get done whenever you are involved with a bureaucracy. Be patient.

When you are filing a claim with the government for support, as you are not able to work anymore; be aware that the government is going to try very hard to discourage you from pursuing your claim. The younger you are, the harder that they will try to discourage you.

After all, they are losing money. First off, they will lose the money that they will have to pay out to you if your claim is successful. Secondly, they won't be getting another dime from you in income taxes. Nobody, not even the government, likes to lose money.

Give your police department and their officers respect. They are there to protect the public, and you cannot begin to imagine the number of ways that they are called upon to do this. It is a very difficult job and they generally try to do it the best way they can. There is an awful lot of stress associated with their job; and it sometimes seems like a miracle to me that they are generally as polite as they are. Those people, if they are good officers, often get very frustrated with the system; but they obey the rules that they are given to work with.

Our Systems

The systems we have
Suck, 'tis true.
But 'til we fix 'em,
We gotta make do.
We have to work
To change what's wrong.
I warn you though,
It takes quite long.
Use your voice
And your vote;
That's the only way,
Bosses take note.

Growing Up

Many people have a lot to say about what defines a man and don't say a single word about what defines a woman. Apparently they feel that the presence of breasts and menstruation defines the difference between womanhood and girlhood. They are only partially correct.

The true difference between manhood and boyhood is the same as the difference between womanhood and girlhood. The presence of secondary sexual characteristics simply shows the physical maturation of the person. It does not have anything to do with the emotional maturation of the person which is adulthood. You are an adult when you are willing to take responsibility for all your actions and the consequences thereof.

If you feel that your physical maturation into adulthood has made you into an adult, you are dead wrong. Your displays of courage, physical strength, willingness to fight, or sexual attractiveness to the opposite sex do not make you into an adult.

When you start taking care of your responsibilities, such as getting yourself up in time for school, doing your homework without being prodded by your parents, helping with the common chores around the house, you are showing signs of emerging adulthood. You have to be willing to accept the consequences of your actions, without trying to get out of it, to be considered an adult in my eyes.

A lot of people, especially young people, seem to be suffering from the delusion that the world, or their parents, owes them a living. Nothing could be further from the truth; not even the notion that the world is flat! Yes, your parents are responsible to take care of you when you are a child; but, as an adult, it is your responsibility to take care of yourself.

Generally, your responsibilities grow as you age. As a baby, your responsibilities don't even include wiping your own rump. As a six year old, you are expected to dress yourself and be able to eat by yourself. By the time you are a teenager, you should be helping with the common chores around the house.

Your privileges are supposed to grow at the same rate as your responsibilities. This helps to teach you that with responsibility comes privilege. First you have to prove that you will take care of your responsibility, then you get the privilege. I am certainly not going to tell you that it happens that way all the time; as I would hate to see you die laughing, but that is the way that it is supposed to work.

To My Son

Man high you've grown,
Straight and tall;

And you think
I know nothing at all.
You will learn,
Soon I hope,
Your father is not
Such a dope.
Mouthy, you are,
And foolish too;
But I was once
That way too.
Time will teach you
What I cannot.
Your elders have wisdom;
Believe it or not.

Health

Try to ensure that you get enough sleep. You can get by with less sleep than you need, but it takes a toll on your body.

Do not abuse your body, take care of it. If you do not take care of it by getting enough exercise and sleep, your body will not function as well, nor will you live as long as you could have.

It is far better to release tension as laughter then as anger. It is also far healthier and much better for everyone around you.

It will pay you to follow your doctor's advice. You will tend to live a lot longer.

Always get a second opinion if you have been diagnosed with a serious condition.

Do not expect your doctor to be perfect, nor always right. You are not, so how can you expect them to be.

Leaving Home

Up until now, you have been in a safe, protected environment. When you leave home, you are in for a rude shock. The world does not care that you forgot, you lost the money, or that you goofed. What they care about is results. If you do not produce the results that are expected of you, expect trouble of one sort or another.

The old fashioned idea of hope chests for girls was a good idea. It embodied the belief that you should plan ahead for your future. This is still a good idea.

Build your future by taking small steps. The first thing is school. This has already been started for you when you were young. Then obtain your driver's license. Next, you need a job so you will have money when you need it. You might need further training in order to obtain a good paying job. Go get that training. Now, go after that good job.

Sometime during these steps, you obtain reliable transportation. You also start acquiring the things that you are going to need when you have a place of your own. You are going to need dishes, silverware, cookware, bedding, and other things.

After that, it is time for you to go get your own place. This sort of thing is kind of like a chess game. You set things up and get everything ready before you try something. Then you will have a much easier time of it.

You have been following this same strategy most of your life. For proof of this, just look at how babies develop. First, they learn to communicate their needs and wants to their parents. For example, they cry, and mom or pop, comes to see what they need or want. Then they start trying to get around by crawling. Then they take another small step, learning to do something else. Eventually, after a lot of small steps, they become an adult.

The same type thing happened in the beginning of a lot of the multi-million dollar fortunes around today. Those people started out very small and gradually built up. They protected themselves against financial setbacks, because if they didn't, unless they were very lucky indeed, they would lose everything that they had built up. Try to follow the same strategy in your life.

When you are ready to move out of the house, be certain that you have enough money stashed away for your initial needs. In addition to the rent and the deposit, you will probably need money for turning on utilities and the phone service. You will also need furniture, bedding, dishes, cookware, and various other things to start out with. Heavens to Murgatroyd, you are even going to have to pay for your own groceries!

Before you commit yourself to a new apartment, check out the area that it is in. There is many an area that seems to be fine in the daytime, but feels very dangerous at night. Remember, you are going to be living there all the time, not just in the daytime.

After you get a telephone in your home, do not let your neighbors and friends use your phone without your supervision. Sooner or later, and probably sooner, someone is going to try to take advantage of your hospitality and abuse the privilege by making a lot of long distance calls or accepting collect calls on your phone.

If that happens, when you get the phone bill, you will have a rude shock. Instead of the amount that you have budgeted for, you now have a phone bill of gigantic proportions, which you may well not be able to pay. It doesn't matter to the phone company who ran up your bill, you are still responsible for paying it.

When you move into a new place, take your time before you decide to trust your neighbors, especially the ones who seem very friendly right away. Those are the ones to be most suspicious of. Now, not everyone is a thief, not even most people, but you do have to be careful. Not everyone can be trusted. Thieves often want to scope out your place to see what you have that is worth stealing before they decide to break in. The easiest way for them to do this is to be friendly with you.

Remember, it is very easy for your neighbors to know when you are there and when you are not at home. This makes it easy for them if they decide to break in and rip you off.

The risk of having your home broken into is generally higher both when you are moving out of your old place and when you have just moved into a new place, especially if you are changing neighborhoods. Be very careful at those times.

Once you have left home, and have been away more than a few months, your home town may seem to have changed when you return. It may not have changed, but your perception of it has changed since you have been away. Growth is slow and not very noticeable while it is happening to you. When you return to familiar surroundings that you have not been to in a while, it tends to show itself more in your attitudes and perception.

When purchasing real estate, go thru a reputable real estate company. It would also be a good idea for you to have a lawyer just to ensure that everything is legal and that no one is taking advantage of you. People have been known to attempt to sell property that they do not have the right to sell. Be especially careful when dealing with land contracts. Be certain to get title insurance as well, just in case something is wrong with the title.

Before you make an offer on a house, have it inspected by a professional home inspector. If you cannot find one in the phone book, which is unlikely, ask a local real estate agent. They normally have a list of them.

It will pay you to do this, as you are not a professional, and they are. Your inspector will be able to spot any problems that you have missed in your inspection. It is a whole lot cheaper to pay their fee then it is to pay for costly repairs later on down the road. This way, you will know what the problems are before you make your decision to purchase that dream house.

It is a good idea to have a utility sink in your house. This saves you from having to use the bathtub for doing things it was not really designed to do.

If you are making or buying a shed, figure about how much space that you will need, then add fifty percent. Rest assured that you will need the additional space.

When you are buying a home, it will always pay you to get one with more space than you think that you will need. A spare bedroom comes in awfully handy at times, and you can always use it for storage until you need it.

Sooner or later, you are going to have to move. It is always a pain in the tail, but it can be made easier. Make sure that your stuff is organized and put labels on each side of your boxes. Put everything that you are going to need as soon as you get there in special boxes and load those boxes in last. This includes ashtrays, a small lamp, basic cooking and eating utensils, and your important papers.
You are going to be exhausted when you have finally moved everything into your new place. You will have very little energy left to unpack things, so plan accordingly.

It is a wise idea to keep emergency supplies on hand. Even in the city, the power can go out, and you may have no electricity for hours or even a few days. Having emergency candles or an oil lamp or two will really save the day then.

Keep some food on hand that doesn't need to be cooked and a few gallons of water as well. You might well need them sometime. Keeping a windup alarm clock as a backup alarm really pays off as well. If the power goes off during the night, you will still be able to get up in time to make it to work without being late.

In rural areas, especially in the snow belt, it is always a good idea to have a backup heat source. Kerosene heaters come in very handy when there is no electricity to run your furnace, and you can do some limited cooking on them as well.

<u>Presents</u>

Presents!
Oh, these presents,
I get them every day,
And every one
Requires work,
To banish it someday.
Now I know why,
My parents said
"You have it easy here."

66

If only,
I had listened;
These bills would not come here.

Marriage

Before you get married, think long and hard about it. It is a major decision and it will have a major impact on your life in the long term. Even just living together will have a very significant effect on your life.

If you do not want to be with your special person twenty-five hours a day, eight days a week, thirteen months out of the year, do not marry that person.

Before you decide to marry someone, look carefully at all their faults and virtues. Make sure that their pluses heavily outweigh their minuses, and that you will be able to live with their faults. You are not going to be able to change their flaws, so you had better be prepared to live with them.

Over two hundred years ago Benjamin Franklin wrote this advice: "Keep your eyes wide open before marriage, and half shut afterwards.". It is still good advice.

I do not have to like your prospective mate. Your mother does not have to like them. This is your choice to make, not ours.

It might be a good idea, however, to find out exactly why we don't like him or her. Your parents have had a little more experience with people than you have, up to this point. We just might see something about them that you, blinded by love, don't see.

Before you rush to his or her defense, try to think about the reason why we don't like that person. It is possible that we are wrong, but it is also possible that we are right, too.

Do not go into marriage thinking that you are going to be able to change your partner's faults. This will not happen, so you are setting yourself and your partner up for major trouble in the future.

He or she may change; but it will not be your doing, but the result of maturing and/or a desire on their part to change. You cannot make someone want to change. They have to make that decision on their own.

When it is getting close to your wedding day, it is extremely normal to feel pre-wedding jitters. You may look for a way to bail out of the relationship. Perhaps you might be tempted to cheat on your proposed partner, or take off when you are waiting at the altar. Do not make this mistake. Instead, talk it over with a trusted friend or two, especially one that is already married, and thus can understand what you are going through.

If you didn't have doubts about what you are about to do, you wouldn't be human. Marriage is a very big step for any person. To my mind, it is kind of like jumping out of a perfectly good airplane with a parachute on. Even though you are doing what you want to do, it is still scary.

Sex is a part of the marital relationship, however it is not the major part. You can have a good marriage even if you and your partner are not all that sexually compatible. It merely requires compromises on both of your parts, which is part of a good marriage in the first place.

Marriage or any long term relationship takes a lot of hard work, almost none of it physical. You absolutely have to talk to your partner, especially about the little things that irritate the other partner. You will both have to compromise with each other in these and other areas of your life together.

Marriage is a team effort. You need to work together to achieve your common goals. It takes time, patience, and compromise to learn how to do this.

When you are married, there are going to be some things that you are better at, and some things that your partner is better at. Don't be too proud to admit that they are better at handling a particular task than you are. Let them handle that task and you handle the task that you are better at.

Make sure that you both communicate with each other on what is being done, though. If you don't, things are liable to get fouled up. For example, what happens if the partner that is handling the finances gets in a car accident? They may be dead or severely injured, and now you have to take care of everything and you have no idea what your financial situation is.

This is not a good situation to be in, especially when you are worried near to death about them.

You are going to have the opportunity to have an affair, sooner or later, while you are married. It is up to you to decide what you want to do, but remember to weigh the risks against the potential gains. I suggest that you think this through before you are tempted, as any decisions that you make while you are influenced by passion are not to be trusted.

A friend of mine, who helped me, as a test reader of this book, suggested that I add in this bit of advice: Never go to bed, or sleep, angry at each other. It will only fester, during your rest. Even if you are still upset with your partner, tell them that you love them, before closing your eyes. She feels that you will never regret doing this.

I tend to agree with this, though I don't think that I ever practiced it during my marriages. Perhaps that is one of the reasons that they failed.

I cannot say that this is my advice, as I did not think of it. However, she's been married fifty-five plus years to the same person. I think that her advice is worth listening to, and thinking about.

<u>Marriage</u>

Marriage is
A lifelong venture.
It can be
A grand adventure.
Choose your companion
With some care;
For they will see
You all bare.
You'll both need to talk
And set up rules.
This will keep you
From looking like fools.
You will indeed
Make mistakes.

Admit you're wrong,
For goodness sakes.
"Forgive and forget",
This is divine;
And it will help
Your marriage to shine.

Money

I do not define success in terms of money. I define it by what I have done in this world. Your life may be a financial disaster, but if you have made a positive difference in people's lives, then **to** my mind, you have been a success.

True wealth is not defined in monetary terms. It is defined by the friends and family that you have and the good that you have done.

Money is simply a very rough estimate of the value of the work that one has done. Do not overvalue it. Many a person has done a lot of work in their life and has not a penny to show for it, but has not wasted what little money has come into their hands.

It does not pay to be greedy for money. Yes, it can buy you a lot of nice things; but, how much do you really need as opposed to how much that you want.

Do not waste your money gambling for high stakes. That is simply a way of showing off that you have money to burn. There are much better ways to use your money if you have so much of it.

It does not pay to flaunt the fact that you have a lot of money. It not only makes people jealous (which is what you may intend), but it also makes you a target for thieves.

If you are buying new furniture, do not buy the cheap stuff. Purchase good quality furniture. I have seen a good quality sofa bed last twenty years, in a house with four very active boys growing up, and still be in fairly decent shape. A cheap one, I highly doubt, would have lasted as long as five years, especially as rambunctious as my brothers and I were.

This applies to most things. Get the quality merchandise. It will cost more, but it will be well worth it in the long run. If you buy the cheap stuff, be aware that it probably won't last very long. Most likely, it won't work very well for what you have in mind, either. In the end, you are going to end up paying more than you would have if you had bought quality merchandise in the first place.

It will pay you to shop smart. Always check the ad prices and compare prices in other stores before you make a major purchase. It will really make you feel like an idiot if you discover that you could have bought the same item for fifty or a hundred dollars less if you had just shopped around a bit.

Check the sale prices in the advertising from your competing grocery stores. You can often save a lot of money just by going to another store. Also, use the coupons that are often in the Sunday newspaper or the store advertising paper. That will help you save money as well. Try to purchase the stuff that you use all the time (like toilet paper) in bulk, especially when it is on sale.

Money

Money is important,
I know it's true.
But you must own it;
And not it, you.
It is used
To supply your needs;
But don't let it
Create any greeds.
New things are nice,
I will say this;
But they cannot
Supply you bliss.
Use what you need,
And save the rest;
Then you'll be doing
What is best.

Morals

Look thoroughly at what you have been taught about right and wrong and think about it. Look at all the religious systems of ethics and think about them. Then, establish your own code of ethics and follow it.

The one thing that is absolutely vital to your life is self respect. If you do not respect yourself, you can never like yourself and that is absolutely necessary.

You cannot change your past actions, and you may not like yourself because of those past actions. You can however, decide to change.

You will have to deal with the consequences of your past actions. If you have done wrong to someone, try to make amends.

If you have decided to change, base your liking of yourself upon your new actions, not upon your past ones. You will undoubtedly stumble and fall a few times. This is perfectly normal and signifies nothing more that you are a fallible human being, not that you are beyond all hope of redemption and can never change.

Have you ever watched a baby when it is trying to learn to walk? They stumble and fall down a lot, then they pick themselves up and try again. Yes, they do cry sometimes when they fall down, but they do not give up.

You are in the same type situation that the baby is, so do like he does. Pick yourself back up and keep trying. This sort of thing does take time, just like the baby does not learn to walk in five minutes. Be patient with yourself, results will come with time and effort.

At the end of each day, sit down somewhere that you will not be disturbed and judge your actions of that day. What did you do right and what did you do wrong? How can you keep from making those mistakes again? If you do that without fail, you will be a much better person and you will like yourself a whole lot better.

It has long been said that honesty is the best policy. I agree with that saying. In the short run, it often gets you into trouble, especially if you do not have much tact. In the long run, however, it pays enormous dividends.

Honesty is very important. I cannot stress how important it will be in your life. It will affect the number and types of jobs available to you throughout your life, for one thing. If you are not known as honest, how will people trust you with important jobs that they have available.

For instance, if you are known as a dishonest person, you will not be able to get a cashier job, or a job in a bank, or in any trusted position. You will not be able to be bonded or have a security clearance, for another matter. It will be much more difficult to get credit if you are known to be dishonest. After all, if they cannot trust you, why should they lend you money?

Always do your top level best in whatever you do. You will have less to regret later on.

I know that a lot of people lie, but I do not want you to do so. Lying tends to cause you very serious problems. In the long run, those problems are much more serious than the problem that you are trying to solve by lying your way out of.

First off, if you always tell the truth, people that know you will know this and will believe you when you tell them something that is very difficult to believe. Sooner or later, there will come a time in your life when this is going to happen.

Secondly, a reputation for truthfulness goes hand in hand with honesty. You cannot be honest while you are lying.

Thirdly, words have power. I know that this is hard for you to believe, but it really is true. Every time that you lie, you diminish the power in your spoken words. It also diminishes the trust that people will put in you. After all, if you are going to lie to them, why should they trust you?

There is nothing wrong with partying, but make sure that you do so safely. Make sure that there is a designated driver who will get you and all your party home safely. Otherwise, don't get drink.

If you do not mean an apology, do not say it.

When you are engaged in a long term struggle with an enemy, there is always the possibility that, in your efforts to destroy that enemy, you will become just like him. Guard yourself against that. Examine your proposed actions from a moral standpoint, not just from the standpoint of whether it will help you destroy him or not.

It is extremely easy to rationalize to yourself that what you want must also be what is right and proper, especially when you are in a position of power. Try very hard not to fall into that trap. That is one of the ways that power corrupts people.

Always guard yourself against your weaknesses. For example, if you are currently or usually in financial difficulties, it is a very bad idea to take a position as a treasurer of any organization.

Do not feel alone in this, there are all things that we do not trust ourselves with. A case in point, if someone were to ask me to hold onto a lottery ticket worth a million dollars or more, considering my normal financial difficulties; I would not trust myself. I would be extremely tempted to cash that ticket in myself, and betray their trust in me.

Never betray your principles, especially for money. I do not use the phrase "mere money" because the amount usually involved seldom can be classified as "mere". Usually it is a large sum to you. However large it is, it is never worth the amount of self-respect that you will lose. You will also be losing a large amount of sleep due to the sleepless nights you are going to be having in the future.

Respect

Learn to respect
Other's rights,
And you'll avoid
A lot of plights.
Think of that,
Before you act;
You'll have less trouble.
That's a fact.
Life is rough
Enough indeed,
Without causing trouble
By misdeeds.

Paperwork

I know that it is a pain in the arse to do paperwork. I hate doing it myself. However, today's society requires quite a bit of paperwork to be done. NEVER put it off, just get it done as quickly as possible.

Make sure that it is accurate, though. Otherwise, you will eventually have to fill out yet more paperwork correcting your mistakes.

Deal with your business mail promptly and file it away in an organized fashion. Don't just toss it in a pile to be filed away later; it will get lost.

Keep your stuff, especially any important papers or files, organized. Otherwise you will spend many an anxious hour hunting for what you need.

Parenthood

Once your child starts asking you questions, you will learn how many things there are that you don't know anything about.

Sooner or later, you are going to have responsibility for a young child, if only for a few hours. Do not assume that they have the knowledge of this world to keep them safe that you do. They do not. They are just learning about this world and it is your responsibility to keep them safe.

If they are at all mobile, especially when they have just learned to crawl, keep both eyes on them. Do not let them out of your sight. It is very easy for them to get into trouble and get hurt, and it can happen in the blink of an eye, it seems like.

Having a child changes everything in your life, so think carefully before you bring a child into this world. Even if you acquire a child by becoming a stepparent, your whole life is going to change drastically.

If you bring a child into this world, you have a duty to that child to take care of it and protect it. Sometimes you may not be able to. Sometimes you may have to sacrifice what you want to do, in order that your child gets what he or she needs. You must make your decisions based upon the best interests of that child, not upon your wishes.

I believe it was Sir Francis Bacon that wrote: "He that hath a wife and children hath given hostages to fortune." He was very correct. You now must think of them and their welfare before you make any decisions, particularly major ones.

When you are making a decision about your child, always act in the best interests of your child. Do not base it in your best interests, but in the welfare of your child. We are all human, and we all make mistakes. I can absolutely guarantee that you too, will make a decision, that, in the light of time, will prove to have been a terrible, perhaps tragic mistake.

When this happens, and it <u>will</u>, if you acted in what you believed to be the best interests of your child, you will have little to reproach yourself with. You made the best decision that you could, with the information available
to you at the time. It will still haunt you, but you will not have nearly as much sense of guilt that you would have if you had acted selfishly.

Quite often, if an unmarried woman gets pregnant, she chooses not to inform the other party concerned. If she chooses to have an abortion, that is her right. However, if she decides to bear that child, the father should be informed. Both of you have decisions to make, not just one party.

If you become pregnant, especially if you are not married, you are going to have to do some very serious thinking about the situation. It is time to make some hard decisions, and you must take into account the baby's welfare.

Basically, you have three options; have an abortion (where that is legal), have the baby but give it up for adoption, or raise the child. It is your body, so it is your decision (on abortion);

however you should take into account your partner's opinion as well.

If you have gotten someone pregnant, you are going to have to do some serious thinking, as well. It is her body, so it is her right to decide as to whether or not to have an abortion.

If she decides to have the baby, the decision is now as to who is going to be raising that child. You do, in most places, have some input into that decision. In any event, if you decide not to become a father, you still have an option. You may go to court and give up your parental rights. Quite often, you have not been told about this right, but you should know that you have that option. It is not something to exercise lightly.

In my experience, most men have never been made aware of this alternative to parenthood, while almost all women have been advised of this possibility. This, to my mind, is wrong. Both sexes need to be aware of all the alternatives available to them.

I must warn you though, that you may have a fight on your hands if you choose to terminate your parental rights. At least in the USA, it seems to me that the laws and the courts are not as willing to terminate a father's parental rights (and all that lovely child support money!) as they are to terminate a mother's rights. Other countries may well have more sensible laws.

If a child is born, you both have a duty to see that it is taken care of properly. If you choose not to raise that child, then turn him or her over to the proper authorities. Do not just abandon the child by leaving him or her in a dumpster or some such place.

Even if you will get in trouble with your parents or someone else if they find out that you have given birth, please make sure that the baby is properly taken care of. It is much better for you to suffer harsh words, or even beatings, than for that child to suffer neglect, or possibly even death. You can protect yourself a whole lot better then that baby can protect him/herself.

When a man emotionally realizes and accepts responsibility for taking care of or supporting another person, they tend to work longer and harder at their job. This does not necessarily happen at the time when they legally accept responsibility, but when deep down inside them, they accept it.

When a woman emotionally realizes and accepts the responsibility of taking care of another person, they tend to focus very highly on that person. This generally happens after they have borne a child, but not always.

It does take time for both sexes to emotionally accept these new responsibilities, but it usually takes women less time, because it is kind of shoved in their face. Pain tends to focus a person's attention; and when she has that long agony of childbirth and a baby put in her arms afterwards, that does tend to get her attention, deep down inside.

Do not spoil your child. It can be very hard to do this, especially when they start crying, but don't give in. It is much better for him or her to learn at an early age that he or she does not get to get his way in everything. They are not the center of the universe and do not rule the roost. You are in charge, not them.

If you do not make sure that they know this, you are not doing them any favors and you are setting both yourself and them up for some very hard times later on in life. A spoiled two year old can be cute, but a spoiled fifteen year old most definitely is not.

If they are convinced that they cannot possibly do anything wrong and that anything that they want should be theirs, they may well end up in prison or dead later in life. At the very least, they are going to have some very rude shocks when they go out into the world on their own.

"Divide and conquer" is a very old and effective strategy. Children tend to attempt to apply it to their parents at a very young age. Do not let it happen to you. Back up your fellow parent.

Remember, your children are going to look at you as an example of what they should do and how they should behave. Make sure that you set them a good example.

Make sure that you make time to be with your child on their important occasions. Remember, they are only young once.

As a parent, you are going to have enormous power over your child. Think a great deal about how you are going to guard yourself against abusing that power. There will be a lot of opportunities over the years for you to abuse the power that you have over your child. Guard against it, and stop yourself! You will harm your child in a way much worse than mere physical abuse is able to accomplish.

In the years to come, there are going to be many times when you will have to have to let your child make their own mistakes and learn from them. This is going to be one of the hardest tasks that you, as a parent, will have.

It is like teaching them to walk or ride a bike. You know that they are going to fall down and get hurt, sooner or later. You still have to let them go to try it on their own, though. All you can do is to be there for them when they get hurt. Then, they can be your little child again, to care for and fuss over. Sooner or later, though, they are going to be ready to go out and face the world again; and you are going to have to let them go.

It is going to be very hard for you to do this, but you have to let them go. You cannot keep them a child, they have to grow up, whether you like it or not.

After you become a parent, I can guarantee that you are going to have some sleepless nights. You will be wondering if you said the right thing to him/her. Perhaps you will be wondering if you made the correct decision regarding their welfare. All that you can do is to do the best that you can, and learn from your mistakes.

Out of my experience, I can tell you that these nights will tend to happen more often as your child gets older and closer to being an adult.

Teenagers have a nasty habit of thinking that they own the joint and that they can do what they please in your house. Do try not to kill them; remember you were once one yourself and your parents didn't kill you. Extend your teenager the same courtesy.

Every child incurs a debt to their parents for taking care of them while they are young. The interest on this debt is paid by taking care of the stuff that your parents are unable to do because of physical disabilities, and by taking care of them when they are no longer able to care for themselves. The principal is paid by caring for your children, teaching them right from wrong, and helping them to find their way in this world.

Try to make the payments.

You do not have to love your stepchildren in order to successfully raise them. You do, however, have to care about them and what happens to them. You also have to show them that you care, whether they like you or not.

Parenthood

The hardest task
I think I know;
A parent has
Is letting go.
Standing back
To let them try,
Trying so hard
Not to cry;
You know they're heading
For a fall;
While they're walking,
Oh, so tall.
They must learn
On their own,
Now that they
Are fully grown.
All we can do
Is give advice,
And pray they don't

Fall on ice.
We know they must
Stand on their own;
But, Oh it hurts
To hear them moan.
We pick 'em up,
And patch 'em too;
Sometimes they even
Thank us, too.
We try so hard.
We hope and pray.
When they pull stunts,
Our hair turns grey.
Someday they'll learn.
We hope, real soon;
Right now, they're acting
Like a loon.

Problems

Life is not fair. Do not expect it to be as it just plain isn't and you will be severely disappointed.

You will face a certain amount of injustice in your life. Everyone does, not just you, although it will seem so at the time. What matters is how you deal with it.

Do not depend on other people to help you. They may not always be willing or able to help you.

You are always going to have problems in your life, so get used to it. Even if you won the lottery tomorrow, you would have problems. Now, mind you, your immediate money worries, like how to get enough money to pay the rent and the bills, would be done with; however, you would now have a new level of problems to deal with.

Believe it or not, it would be probably be a worse level of problems to deal with, and one that you are poorly prepared for.

Do not ask other people for help until you have tried everything that you can to solve the problem yourself.

Do not expect help from anyone else in solving your problems. If you get it, be grateful and remember to return the favor. But essentially, it is your problem, and so the solution is your responsibility.

It does not pay to run away from your problems, whatever they are. They are there for you to solve and learn from. Until you solve those problems, they will always be waiting for you.

Usually, if you run away from your problems, the problems just get bigger. Either that, or you tend to add additional problems to your burden, like alcoholism or drug addiction. Either way, it isn't any fun at all.

It sometimes helps to take a break from problems for a quick minute. Take one day off, just <u>one</u> (not a week or a month) and go have some fun, it will relax you. It often also helps you to gain perspective about your problem. However, do not use any kind of drugs or alcohol to get away from it. That is an extremely bad idea and will tend to add more problems on top of your original problem.

Sooner or later, you are going to be chewed out and told that you acted like a complete idiot. Don't feel too bad. We all get that lecture, at least once in our lives. Just make sure that you learn from your mistake.

Know your capabilities. It can be disastrous to overestimate your ability at something and very expensive when you have to call in an expert to fix what you have screwed up.

I have found that reading the daily comic section in the newspaper really helps to deal with the stress in your life. It helps you keep a sense of perspective about your problems. In addition to this, you are liable to laugh like hell when reading some of the comics. Laughter is very healthy for you, and will add a great deal to your enjoyment of life.

You will have trouble in your life. I guarantee that sooner or later something totally unexpected will come up that you have not planned for. This is the way that life is. Sooner or later, you are going to be handed a batch of lemons when you planned on a bushel of apples and your life is going to change.

Just remember, when a door closes in your life, there will be another one opening for you. It will take time and trouble to find that door, but I promise you, there is one.

It is ok to feel sorry for yourself. Go ahead and indulge yourself, for half an hour at the most. Then look around and start figuring out how you can make your life better.

There are going to be times when you are going to have to continue to function even though you are not feeling well. Perhaps you have a severe toothache or are sick. Hang in there, this happens to everyone sooner or later. Just watch your temper, as when a person is not feeling well, they tend to get angrier a lot quicker.

It is a much better idea figuring out how to improve your situation than to waste your time and energy complaining about it. There is almost always something that can be done to improve your situation. Try working on that, instead of complaining so much. You will feel much better about yourself.

There is always someone in a worse situation than you are in. Even if you are living on the street, there is someone who is having a harder time than you are. Therefore, accept what you do have and work to make your situation better. Do not give up, you can make your life better. You may have to work like hell to make it better, but it can be done.

Trouble

Pedaling home,
One summer's eve;
A skunk perfumed
The evening breeze.
Slow down I did,
And did it right quick;
For that skunk's ire
Was raised to the quick.
Soon I beheld
That luckless wretch.
His distress, did my nostrils,
Thoroughly catch.
I sped myself home
Away from his stench;
And put some stuff
Upon the bench.
Got medicine for him,
And some spare clothes;
For he'd surely
Have to burn all of those.
We talked as he bathed
In the lake nearby;
And burned all his clothes

In the fire's eye.
We talked of our troubles
As people do.
He was really
Feeling blue.
As I went home,
It occurred to me;
That dude has way
More problems than me.

If you think that your life is rough now, try using an outhouse in the middle of winter. There still are people who use exactly that sanitation system to this day. Some people do not even have the luxury of having toilet paper to use.

Do not bother to blame your misfortunes on "Bad Luck". Certainly, random chance plays a larger part in our lives than most people will admit. However, "Luck" usually consists of recognizing or not recognizing the opportunities that random chance presents to us.

A case in point, once I found a hundred dollar winning lottery ticket just lying there on the street. If I hadn't been in the habit of picking up lottery tickets that were laying on the ground, examining them for winners, and putting the losing tickets in the trash; I wouldn't have noticed it.

That would have been "Bad Luck" for me, as I really needed the money at the time. As it was, I had a bit of "Good Luck".

Try your best not to complain about things. If you are unhappy with the situation that you are in, see what you can do about making it better. If that is not possible, endure it with as much grace as you can. Remember, everything changes and eventually the situation that you are in will change, too.

Sooner or later, you are going to make a bad deal and you are going to lose your money on something. Do what you can to recover your money, but don't dwell on it too long. Learn your lesson and move on. It does not pay to dwell forever on it. Remember, too many sour grapes causes indigestion.

I know that lawyers are expensive, but there are times that you can't afford not to have a lawyer working on your behalf. If you are purchasing or selling real estate, getting a divorce, or have gotten involved with the criminal legal system; it is a very good idea to at least consult a lawyer. On occasion, lawyers will give an initial free consultation.

Before you disclose your problem to a lawyer, find out first if he/she is representing any of the other parties to the dispute that you are in. If they are, you had better not discuss it with them and find another attorney.

Never give in to blackmail. It seldom pays off. If they are threatening you with exposure to the police, very quietly get a lawyer and explain everything to your lawyer. He/she may well be able to help you with both the blackmailer and your legal problem.

If they are threatening you with exposure of a secret to someone you love, tell that person all about it. At least it will be out in the open then, and you will not have to try to hide it anymore. Then talk to the police and see what they can do to help.

Remember, blackmail is highly against the law and the police will want to catch that person. You are most certainly going to have some problems, but they will be much less than you will have if you allow yourself to be blackmailed.

I know that it will be extremely tempting, but try very hard not to kill the person that is trying to blackmail you. Let the police handle it. If you murder that person, you are just setting yourself up for a lot more problems instead of solving the problem that you do have.

Into each life,
Some pain must fall.
For some, it seems
It never ends.
Come what may;
You'll find, my friends,
Some other's pain,
Makes yours seem small.

Relationships

Perfection

Perfection is
An unattainable thing;
At least for the person,
That wants more than a fling.
We are not perfect,
Not even close;
So why should we
Expect the most.
What matters more,
Then the shape we wear,

Is the person inside
When all's laid bare.

A person's looks are often the basis of an initial attraction, however their personality is what keeps them attractive to you.

Do not waste your time searching for your perfect partner. You will not find him or her. Very few people are perfect and guess what, you aren't either. With all your flaws, if you found that "perfect" person; why would they want you? They would want someone as perfect as them, in the first place.

If you are interested in a woman that has children but does not have custody of them, be wary. Find out why she doesn't have custody before you get in a serious relationship with her. Does she see her children? Is she paying child support?

Do not necessarily take her word for what happened. Find out what happened. She may be lying to you, and if so there is a possibility of some major character defects within her. Of course, it might just be that she feels that it is none of your business, too.

If you are interested in a man who does not have custody of his children, find out if he is attempting to pay his child support. What type of a father is he? Does he see his children, if not, why not?

Trust is very important in a relationship. If you can't trust them, it is very hard to live with them.

Do not let your romantic interests distract you from your life plans, especially when you are young. Get your career set up first, then worry about serious romance. Many a person has screwed up their life plans because of romance; and yes, it can happen to you, too. The opposite sex will still be there when you have gotten your career on track, and you will be better able to cope with the distractions that they create at that point.

Just because you have had a bad experience with one member of the opposite sex does not mean that all of them are the same way. You have to deal with each person as an individual and not let your past bad memories interfere with your present relationship.

It is ok to be wary, but do not assume that everyone is going to screw you over just because one person did.

Do not be too quick to jump into another relationship just after you have broken up with someone else. Give yourself a bit of time to heal your wounds first.

Looking for Love

Learning to trust;
It's so hard, you see;
When every time
It's been a bust.
Your heart is hurt.
Scared you are,
Of trying again;
And being hurt
Yet again.
Walking alone
Thru this world
Is not bad;
But loneliness always
Makes you so sad.
You see all those couples,
And wonder how come
They found someone;
And yet you have never
Found that special one.
They've learned the lesson
You've yet to learn.
You have to take
A chance for romance.

Do not ever let anyone pressure you into
having sex. You will know when you are ready to
have sex with that person. Just because they are
ready to have sex doesn't mean that you are ready
to. If you tell them no and they keep pressuring
you, then something is wrong with that
relationship.

It is up to you as to what you do, but I suggest that you do not have sex with another person unless you care deeply about that person. I definitely understand the biological pressures, but given the amount of venereal diseases out there, this is a reasonable precaution. This will also tend to make the sex much more meaningful and fulfilling to you.

When you start to have sex, make sure that you use birth control, and I don't mean the rhythm method either. There are still very few choices available for men in that field, but there are a lot of options for women. It is the responsibility of both of you to choose a method that works.

Watching and reading too much erotica tends to jade your appetite for the real thing so use it sparingly.

At some point in a long term romantic relationship, you and your partner need to sit down and establish ground rules for that relationship. Otherwise, you two are going to be getting into a lot of arguments. It is much better to discuss each other's expectations for that relationship and set the rules up beforehand, than to start arguing when the other person does something that you don't like.

When you are in a relationship with someone, sooner or later there will be hurt feelings and an argument between the two of you. When this happens, do your best to fight fair. Do not try to hurt their feelings, just because they have hurt yours. Let them know that they have hurt you and why it hurts you.

You both need to listen to each other. You cannot listen if you are speaking at the same time that they are talking. So take turns talking between yourselves. Agree on a time limit for each of you, say five minutes apiece.

Sooner or later, there will be a time when one or both of you are too pissed off to be able to talk to the other. At that point, it is probably a good idea for the two of you to stop discussing it and do something together without speaking. Go to the park and watch the sunset together, or take a drive in the country.

Anything can work as long as it cools you both off and you are together. If you stay together while you are angry with each other and cool down your tempers together, it reinforces your commitment to each other.

Do not fight with your partner in front of the children. Go into a separate room.

If you find that you are one of the type of people who wants and/or needs to be physically abused by their mate or to abuse their mate; then ritualize it by going into Bondage and Dominance.

Do not just clobber them when you want to, or provoke them into clobbering you.

You both need to sit down and establish ground rules for this sort of behavior. Otherwise, your relationship will go to pieces, very swiftly.

When you are out in public or on the job, you tend to be on your best behavior. When you are at home, you tend to let down your behavior standards. It is very easy to allow your temper to flare up to a much greater extent than you would ever allow it to at work.

Try very hard not to do this. You will get along a lot better with your mate and family.

You cannot ever force someone to love you. Don't even bother to try. Love has to be given freely.

You can force someone to stay with you, but it is not worth it. First off, it is totally and completely wrong, unless you are a parent and responsible for that child. For a short term situation with a child, I can see it. It is not worth it, though, for a long term matter, even if that child is your own.

If that child dislikes you or your actions that much, it would be better for him or her to be with someone who cares about him or her and that he or she cares about. Remember, you are the parent and responsible for that child's welfare.

How will you be able to teach him/her what they need to know if they cannot stand the sight of you? How will you be able to show that child how to love someone else? He/she may well not even be able to recognize that you love them.

Advice to Daughter

Time is fleeting by
I know;
And your heart
Is yearning so.
Love, you fear,
Is passing by;
And you wonder
Why, oh why.
It may well be,
You never know;
But you can help
Prevent it tho.
Your body, you fear,
Is the cause of your plight.
At best, you are
Barely half right.
First, your head

Must be straight;
To be open to love,
Be rid of hate.
Second, you must
Like yourself.
So consider your actions,
And judge yourself.
If you do not
Like what you see;
Then change your actions,
Till you like the new "me".
Third, you must
Be willing to meet.
Open your heart,
And use your feet.
We all have problems;
That you know.
The severest of them,
You must conquer, tho.
Take your time,
And look around.
I guarantee,
Wrong ones abound.
The best are those
Who have a plan;
They may adapt,
And make room for a clan.
It's the small things
That tell the tale;
So watch and see
If he's beyond the pale.
If you do
All of this;

You might well
Find one to kiss.

Religion

Study all the major religious books, regardless
of your religion. If you look carefully, there is a
lot of wisdom hidden inside each of them.

If you look closely at the "Golden Rule" for
each major religion, you will find a lot of
similarity between those rules. Think this through
carefully. Wouldn't this mean that each of those
religions have some validity to them? Therefore,
do not be too eager to say that your religion is the
only true way. It is simply a way that works for
you. Believe it or not, there is more than one way
up the spiritual mountain towards enlightenment.

Our Beliefs

We all have
Our beliefs,
And are positive
They're right.
What if,
Come Judgment Day;
Things start
Getting kinda tight.

Will you be able
To tell the Boss:
"Although I was wrong
In my beliefs;
I caused no one
Any loss."?

Scams

If someone that you have never met before
says that he/she is going to do you a favor, watch
out! That favor is quite likely removing all that
excess weight that you are carrying, like your
money, your clothes, and anything else they find
vaguely valuable.

There are all kinds of scams around to separate
you from your money. Be very wary of them.
Remember, if it sounds too good to be true, it
usually is.

It can be very difficult to scam a person who is
honest, but does not believe that other people
necessarily are.

Some scams are based on confusing you. If
things start to get confusing, slow everything
down until you understand each transaction. If
you don't understand each and every action, stop
immediately! Handle each transaction separately.
Do not let them rush you, not even a little bit.

Another type of scam is based on your desire for love or love of others. Watch out for warning signs. Don't let yourself be deluded.

If someone gives you a set of figures and asks you to make a decision based on those figures; check them out to see if the mathematics and the figures are correct, well before you make a decision. Make sure that all the important factors are included. Often, to deceive you, some important factors are omitted in the figures that you are given.

Remember, figures don't lie, but liars figure.

NEVER sign a blank contract or a blank check!

Always read a contract thoroughly before you sign it. If you do not understand it, do NOT sign it until you do understand it and all the provisions in it. It is often a very good idea to hire a lawyer to check your contract over and explain it to you as necessary. When the contract involves a large amount of money or a large amount of your time, always hire a lawyer.

Sudden Disability

One day, you may find yourself suddenly handicapped and unable to do the things that you are used to doing. This sometimes happens because of a severe accident or illness.

How it happened does not matter nearly so much as how you are going to deal with it. Yes, it is totally unfair that it happened to you; but, life is not fair. Go ahead and grieve for a bit, get it out of your system. Now, get up off of your mental rump, and decide how you are going to deal with it.

Believe it or not, but this happens to all of us. Normally, this situation happens gradually through a process called aging. If you don't believe me, just look at the elderly people in your life. Believe it or not, but they used to be able to do all the stuff that you are used to doing. Now they cannot do that anymore, and neither can you.

What is important for you to focus on is what you can do, not what you can't. Pissing and moaning about your pitiful state is not going to makc your situation any better. What will make it better is your acceptance of the situation, and utilizing every resource that you have available to you. This includes joining a support group, and learning from their accumulated experience and wisdom.

Yes, a door was just closed to you, and closed very rudely, indeed. However, this also means that there is another door opening up for you. You merely have to stop bemoaning your fate, and look around for that opening door. It will most certainly take some time and effort on your part to find that door, but it does exist. I promise you that it is there, if only you will open yourself to the possibility of finding it.

Aging

Getting old,
System failing;
What am I to do?
Responsibilities
Not all met;
What am I to do?
Body's changing,
Going down;
What am I to do?
Searching for
Another door;
What is it
I must do?
Carry on,
And keep on trying,
Without anger
Or regret.
These things happen
To us all.
Why;
We do not know.
There is a reason,

That I know;
Though I do not know it.
Little do we
Know at all;
How our actions
Affect others,
That we have not met.
Rest assured,
They do indeed;
Like ripples
In a pond.
So carry on
And do your best;
With love for one and all.

Survival

People, especially young people, often have a habit of thinking themselves invincible; after all nothing bad could possibly happen to precious, irreplaceable them. Well, it can happen to you. Learn that lesson now, otherwise the School of Hard Knocks will teach you that lesson, and the tuition fees that particular school charges often include yours or other people's lives.

School of Hard Knocks

The School of Hard Knocks
Is not any fun.
You can't cut classes;

You're up with the sun.
The lessons you get
Come so painfully;
You'd prefer to have
Major surgery.
You bust your behind
With so little to show;
You wonder how come
You didn't know;
That this would result
From breaking the rules.
Now you regret
Acting a fool.

Always have a way of escape planned in case of emergency, especially in your home. When you go into a building for the first time, notice where all the exits are, especially the emergency ones. You may have to find your way there in total darkness or in a room filled with smoke.

People, like animals, are creatures of habit. It is a good idea, in terms of security, to change your routines every once in a while. Do not leave or arrive at your home at the same time every day. Vary your route to and from work. This will help keep you a bit safer.

There is absolutely nothing wrong with being scared. You cannot, however, let feeling that way, dictate to you what you will or will not do.

Courage often consists of being scared nearly to death and doing what has to be done anyhow.

There may well come a time when you are going to have to do something that you know is wrong, for the sake of survival. If this happens, do it, but try very hard not to repeat it. It will be easier to do the next time and even easier the times after that. Try to make sure that you are never in a position where you have to do it again after the first time. Otherwise, you may well kill your conscience.

It's a good idea to keep a survival kit in your car, in case of emergencies. Vehicles can break down in the middle of the night, on a lonely road. Car accidents can happen. Trust me, it pays to have one. It doesn't necessarily have to take up a lot of room, but if you choose wisely, there isn't much that you can't do with it, either. A word to the wise, though. Buy good quality stuff, rather than get cheap stuff. Trust me, it pays off.

The most important factor is, however, knowing how to use whatever you have. For example, if you have plenty of matches, but don't know how to build a fire, those matches are absolutely useless to you.

Make time each day for you to relax and unwind. There will be times when you are busy as all get out. This is really when you need the time to relax, most of all, even if it is for only a half hour or so. You will make better decisions the next day if you do. Then you will not make as many mistakes and have to spend more precious time correcting them.

It will not seem so at the time, as you will be just as busy; but you will have been able to accomplish more things. You also won't be as frustrated, which will help keep your level of stress down.

Avoiding Trouble

Walking quietly
Thru this life;
Avoids many
An evil strife.
Do not boast
And shout about;
Or you'll have trouble
With some lout.

Time

Time is the one commodity that we all have. It is a finite amount and we do not know how much that we will have, so do not waste it. Spend your life well.

Make the time every once in a while to watch a sunrise.

Make sure that you take time to have some fun. Life is way too short for you not to have some enjoyment.

When you are going somewhere that you know that you are going to have to wait at once you arrive, take a book or something along to usefully occupy your time. Otherwise, you are liable to get very bored.

Time

Our time can fill
With petty stuff.
Don't let trash
Give you guff.
Earn a living,
You must, 'tis true;
But do not let it
Consume all of you.
Make the time
To have some fun;
And to be with
Loved ones in the sun.

Transportation

Always keep your vehicle in the best shape that you can possibly manage. I do not care if it is a junker or not, do your best to take care of it. Treat it gently, do not abuse it. Give it the best maintenance that you can possibly afford. This will save you a lot of time, money, and aggravation; and it will prolong the life of your vehicle.

Make certain that you check the oil, transmission fluid, brake fluid, power steering fluid, and radiator fluid at least once a week and more often if necessary. This will help alert you to any problems that are starting to occur to your vehicle. It also may well help prevent you from having to have more expensive than necessary vehicle repairs; and may well help save yours and other people's lives.

Even if all that you have for transportation is a bicycle, maintain it properly. Keep the chain oiled, and the tires inflated properly. The better that you maintain it, the better that it will serve you.

Know how to do simple emergency repairs to your vehicle, like changing a flat tire. Keep the tools handy for fixing these problems. It also pays to keep extra fluids in your car, that you might need, like oil, brake fluid, power steering fluid, antifreeze, and transmission fluid.

It will pay you to learn how to do the simple, everyday, preventive maintenance to your vehicle, like changing the oil, and doing a tuneup. It's a lot cheaper to do it yourself, rather than to pay someone else to do it, I promise. A lot of auto parts stores will take care of stuff like used oil and antifreeze for you, if you bring it in to them. Generally the county waste management sites will also do this, as well as take all kinds of stuff, like old furniture, and old chemicals, including old cans of paint.

There will come a time when you will have to decide whether your vehicle is worth putting any more money into or if you should invest in another vehicle instead. Think very carefully about it before you come to a decision.

No matter how well that you maintain it, sooner or later, it is very likely that you are going to have to replace it. It could be due to mechanical failure, or an accident. It doesn't matter. If you aren't planning on how you are going to replace it, and setting funds aside for that, you are going to be in trouble. Never bet that someone is going to be able to bail you out of the trouble that you have created for yourself, by not planning ahead. They might not be able to help, due to troubles of their own.

As you go to check out possible purchases, be very careful. There are a lot of lousy cars out there. Be aware that many a person will try to sell you a vehicle that isn't worth half of what they are asking for it. Remember, no one ever sells a vehicle because it runs too good.

If you are depending on a ride to get you back and forth to some place, be careful. Always have a backup plan just in case something goes wrong. What happens if that person gets mad at you or decides not to give you a ride?

Often, at that point, you may not find out about their decision. They simply don't show up when you expect them to. At that point, you are screwed. Quite often, you may be losing money because of their decision, possibly even your job. This is why I urge you to have a backup plan, already in place.

Perhaps you are riding the bus back and forth to work. What happens if the bus has a breakdown, or you miss it? This is why, if possible, you should take an earlier bus, or set of buses, then you need to. This way, you will make it to work on time, whether the buses are running late or not. Murphy's Law does come into play, often when you least expect it to, or can least afford it to do so.

It will pay you to obey the speed limits. They are established for a reason. Most especially, if the speed limit is much lower than is usual for residential areas, obey it. There is a dangnab good reason for it, especially on curves.

Trust

Never trust someone just because you like them. Trust them when they have proven themselves worthy of trust.

Do not trust someone simply because you care about them. Remember, if you trust someone simply because of a romantic relationship, what happens to the secrets you have told him/her when that relationship breaks up?

If you have betrayed someone's trust, you can regain it sometimes, but it is a long, slow process. First, you have to show them that you regret what you have done. You also have to show them that you are guarding against a repetition of that action.

Never loan money, even to a friend or relative, if you are not prepared to lose it. The first time that you loan it to them is particularly hazardous. This can be one of the ways that you test to see if they are trustworthy or not.

Even if they have repaid you in the past, things can happen that will cause them to be unable to repay you. For instance, what if they get into a bad car accident or are fired from their job? These things happen and it is not always their fault.

If you make a deal with someone, honor that deal. Whether you lose money by going thru with that deal or not, honor it. Believe it or not, the word does get around and you will be more respected by your peers for that. More importantly though, you will respect yourself more for that.

Be very careful about who you let into your car or your home. Many is the person who has given a "friend" a ride while that "friend" is carrying, unbeknownst to them, something illegal.

Then, that "friend", if you are stopped by the police for a traffic ticket or some such thing, hides what he/she was carrying somewhere inside the car. When the police search the vehicle and find that illegal item or items, you, the driver, will get arrested for possession of that illegal stuff while your "friend" gets off scot free.

It has also happened that the person that you let in your house has hidden something illegal in there that they would rather not be caught with, while you have no knowledge of it being there. This can be very dangerous, especially if someone is after your friend for what he/she has taken from them.

Perhaps an enemy of yours wants to hurt you. One effective method for them to use is to hide something highly illegal in your place and then call the police and inform them of it being there. When the cops search your place, guess what, you are going to jail. And for something that you didn't even know was there.

The last two possibilities seldom happen, but they do occur. The first one is the more likely possibility. This is why I want you to be very picky about who you let in your home or your vehicle. I do not want to see anything like that happening to you.

When you are in a bar or at a party with a lot of people around, watch your drink. Do not leave it unattended by someone that you trust. If you do happen to leave it unattended by mistake; do not under any circumstances drink it. I don't care if it is the last one that you can afford, don't drink it!

Many a person has had a little something extra added to their drink and wound up hurt in some fashion because of it. The new fashion is for the "date rape" drug to be added, but it has happened quite often down thru the centuries; not only for robbery, but for other, more evil purposes as well.

<u>Violence</u>

This world can be a very dangerous place. Not everyone in it obeys the law or respects the rights of others. Know how to defend yourself and be prepared to do so at any moment.

Cultivate the ability to always know what is going on around you. It will take a lot of practice to be able to do it well, but it will pay you handsomely to take the trouble. It has kept a lot of people from getting hurt and it might just do the same for you.

If something doesn't feel right about a situation, it probably isn't. Get out of there immediately. Abandon your belongings if necessary, they are worth much less than your life or your health.

Just because you do not want violence, do not make the mistake of assuming that the other person does not want it. This can prove extremely hazardous and sometimes fatal.

All too often, when there is trouble, the police arrive far too late to be able to protect you. Therefore you have to be able to protect yourself and others whom you love. This is not the fault of the police; it is just the way things are. Criminals do not wait to attack you until you have called the police and they have arrived on the scene. For some odd reason, criminals try to avoid the company of police officers, especially when they are committing a crime.

Be aware of how each item in your home can be used to defend yourself. Chairs can be tipped over to trip an attacker. Spices, especially pepper may be used to impede their breathing or vision.

Lamps or other things may be used to clobber your attacker with. The kitchen knives may be used as weapons as well. If you spray perfume in someone's eyes, you may blind them.

Look around your home while you have leisure to do so and think how you may defend yourself in the future. Do not plan exactly what you will do as your attacker is unlikely to do what you have expected him/her to do, just have a general idea of what you can use and then use what is handy and/or usable at the time.

Never use violence except as a last resort. Talking about the problem between you and the other person is usually a whole lot smarter solution.

If you absolutely have to use violence, don't tell the other person what you are going to do to them, just do it. All you are doing is attempting to intimidate them, and it most likely won't work. In addition to this, it just gives them time to plan and execute their own moves.

If you choose to own and/or carry weapons, practice with them. Merely owning and carrying a weapon does not mean that you know how or when to use it. Simply owning a gun does not make you an expert marksman.

If you do not receive some kind of training with that weapon and continually practice with it, it is less than useless to you. In fact, it is more apt to get you or someone you love severely injured than it is to help you. Having a weapon and not knowing how to use it leads to a very dangerous case of overconfidence.

When you get angry, put your weapons away, and don't touch them no matter how mad that you get.

A lot of time, it seems that arguments start over some small thing. Then, feelings of pride and anger often start adding fuel to the fire. You feel hurt and want to hurt back. Neither party wants to admit the possibility that they might be wrong. Then, someone loses their temper and tries to hurt the other party physically. At that point, the fight is on.

An awful lot of domestic assault and murder cases stem from such things. I know it sounds crazy, and it actually is; but a lot of court cases start out from something as trivial as that. Can you imagine having to tell a judge that you killed someone in an argument that started about who gets the last piece of chicken?

So please, when you are in an argument, keep your sense of perspective. Remember how minor the thing that you are arguing over actually is, in the general scheme of things. Is the last piece of chicken, or whose comb it is, actually worth hurting or killing someone over?

Work

"I am severely underpaid and highly overworked." Any Employee

"The exact opposite is actually true." Any Boss

If you can make a reasonable living by doing what you enjoy, do that. If not, find a field where you can make a reasonable living and do what you enjoy on a part time basis until you can make a decent living at it.

When you are starting out, you almost always seem to get a low paying job where you work your rear end off. Do not let it bother you, it happens to most everyone. Just do the top level best that you can at that job and try not to complain too much. This job often leads to a higher paying job within the company.

It is a good idea to set your watch by the time clock at work. That way, you are not as likely to be late for work because of any differences between your clock and the one at work.

It is a wise move to arrive about 15 minutes prior to the time that you are scheduled to work; especially if you are on shift work. This way you can clock in and be updated as to what is going on. Also, it is generally considered unwise to clock in precisely at the time that the preceding shift is leaving. In this fashion, you can avoid being caught in the stampede of everyone leaving at the end of their shift.

A former boss once told me: "Work smarter, not harder." That has to rank among some of the best advice that I have ever received. Get the job done right, but try to find an easier way to get it done.

You are going to get chewed out a lot in life. Get used to it. Try to ignore any personal insults like how stupid you were and focus on learning from your mistake (and/or how your boss wants things done).

There are times when you are going to get chewed out just because the person who is chewing on you has had a bad day or has just been chewed out him/herself. Perhaps they are not feeling well, or are in a bad mood. Hang in there, ignore any personal insults as much as you can, and concentrate on doing what you are supposed to be doing.

Sooner or later, you are going to have to chew someone out. Pull them aside and chew them out privately and do it as tactfully as possible. Focus on what they did wrong and how they can do it properly, not on how dumb or stupid that they are. This saves them embarrassment and helps them learn.

There is nothing wrong with being lazy, IF you use that trait in a productive fashion. Figure out the easiest way to get the job done right, and you will not only save yourself some work; but you will be more efficient. Thus, you can get more work done in the same amount of time. You might also end up getting a bonus from your boss if you can figure out a better, easier, and quicker way for the organization to get a job done.

By the way, an awful lot of inventors have made a lot of money by figuring out an easier or better way to get something done.

When you are trying a new technique to see if it works better than your old one, give yourself time to get used to it. After you are used to it, then compare it to your old one to see which works better for you.

When you do something, take the few extra seconds or minutes needed to do the job right. If you screw the job up, you will have to come back to fix your mistakes. When you are short on time, this really adds to your stress level. Now you are frustrated and mad at yourself; plus you have even less time available to get everything accomplished that you need to.

Someone once said that you can get a lot more accomplished if you don't care who gets the credit. He was right. If you concentrate on working together and getting the job done, it will go a whole lot easier. If everyone works together and helps each other out as needed, the day's work tends to run much smoother. If everyone has a sense of humor, it helps too.

Make sure that you do your fair share and a bit more, of the work that your group has to accomplish. Also, help out the other people in your group by giving the new people the benefit of your experience and a helping hand when needed. This will help make you a valued member of that group.

If your boss gives you a task to do that is not normally part of your job, don't argue about it. Just do it, it will most likely take less time than arguing about it will. Besides, just how likely are you to win the argument in the first place?

To better understand how your job fits into the scheme of things at your company, study the corporate mission statement. If they do not have one, which is not unusual at a small company, think of what it would be. Then consider how your job helps them accomplish that mission.

When you are on the job, act professionally. Do not allow your personal problems to affect your performance. I know that this can be very hard to do, just do your best at it.

Pay attention to what you are doing, especially if what you are doing is boring or routine. Any time that you are performing tasks that have become routine to you, that is a time when you are very liable to have an accident. This is because you tend to forget safety precautions. I once knew a woman who nearly sliced her finger off, while she was cutting a watermelon. She wasn't paying attention to what she was doing and allowed herself to become distracted. It can happen to you too, so always pay attention.

Always pay attention to safety!!! When you are on an emotional high or low, this is a prime time for accidents to occur. Another prime time is when you are really moving fast to get things done. Take the extra minute or two to make sure that you are doing it the safe way. Trust me, it will pay off. You will not notice it paying off, but if someone gets hurt, you most certainly will notice that. I do not want you to pay for your inattention to safety with a broken or amputated limb, whether it is yours or someone else's limb. Believe it or not, it can easily happen.

There will be times when you are working your tail off at your job and you will wonder if all that work is worth the little bit of money that you are being paid. Don't quit! Just hang in there, and if you decide later on that it is not worth it, then find another job. Do not just up and walk off of your job. You are simply making a bad situation worse if you do that. Instead of having a little money coming in, you won't have any money coming in if you walk off. Plus, it will be harder to find future jobs, as walking off of your job will be on your record from now on.

If you are unhappy in your job, it will show up in your productivity and in the quality of the work that you do. It is always hard to do at that point, but try to do the best job that you can, regardless.

If you happen to get a minimum wage job, try to make sure that it is not on the day shift. If you are working second or third shift, you have time in the daytime to go out and find a better job. If you are working day shift, you don't have that luxury. You have gotten yourself into a trap.

If you want to go out and find a better job, when you are on day shift, that means that you will likely have to take time off from work. There are two problems with this. First off, your boss quite probably won't like you taking a lot of time off from work, especially to go find another job. Secondly, when you are making minimum wage, it is extremely difficult to afford to take time off from work.

Sooner or later, you are going to get a job that is not right for you. When this happens, try to learn from the experience. Analyze what parts of the job were suited for your talents and what parts weren't. Then try and find a job that is more in line with your skills and talents. Hopefully, you will find another job before you quit or get fired.

Almost everyone gets fired at least once in their lives. When it happens, if you don't know why, politely ask your boss why you were fired. Gather up your things, and depart peacefully. There is no sense in making a scene and it will hamper your ability to get another job. After you calm down, think objectively about why you were fired. Resolve to make sure that the problem doesn't reoccur in your next job. Then, go get another job.

One day, you may find yourself in a job where everyone seems to be harassing you. If it is just in fun, that is one thing. Unfortunately, sometimes it isn't just in fun.

What is probably happening is that no one likes you or they don't like the way that you work. They are trying to make you feel so uncomfortable with that job that you will quit. If that happens to you, probably the best thing that you can do is to go find another job as quickly as possible.

Please remember, however, that most shop workers have a rude, crude sense of humor and everyone gets harassed once in a while. It is just for fun and to make a boring job a little easier to bear. The new workers really get harassed until they show that they can do the job and everyone gets used to them. So, before you quit, make sure that it is not just being done in fun.

Generally, bosses do not like to see you standing around. If there is nothing else to do, clean up the area that you work in. I have found that they tend to get angry if they see you just standing around while waiting for repairs to be done, or waiting for parts to be brought in.

Quite often, there will be someone that you don't get along with at your job. I have found that it is generally best to always be polite to these people and deal with them as little as possible. Be professional about it, and do your best to cooperate with them. You have both been hired in order to get a job done. Focus your attention on that.

Some people are really rude and tend to pick on the people that they dislike. Usually, in this case, they are trying to irritate you. They want to make you uncomfortable and unhappy. Ignore their antics as much as possible, and concentrate on the job at hand.

If necessary, go to your supervisor and complain about it. It may take several times to get anything done, but hang in there. Just concentrate on getting the job done. Sometimes, you can ask for a transfer to another department if the company that you work for is big enough.

It is generally a bad idea to get involved romantically with someone at work. I know that you tend to meet a lot of new people when you get a new job and one or more of them you may well find attractive; however getting involved with one of them will tend to distract you from your main objective, i.e. earning a living.

In addition to that, what happens if the relationship hits a trouble spot or breaks up entirely? You will tend to be fighting with each other instead of cooperating to get the job done as you both should be doing. Even if everything goes well, you will both tend to be distracted from your job.

Sexual harassment does happen on the job and it is just plain wrong! If someone that you don't like makes advances to you and you tell them no, and they accept that, that is one thing. To my mind, that is not sexual harassment. If they don't accept that and keep making advances towards you; then, to my mind, that is sexual harassment. That sort of thing can be hard to prove because it usually happens when no one else is around.

Sexual harassment takes many forms. In any form, it is wrong. I have always felt it best to keep my sex life and my working life separate.

That way, sexual jealousy cannot possibly rear its ugly head on the job and cause problems. Other people feel differently about this.

There will be times when you give a fellow employee a ride to or from work. If it is just once in a while, that is okay; but if it becomes a habit make sure that you insist on gas money. They are taking up your time and constraining your actions before and after work.

For example, what if you wanted to go somewhere after you get out of your job? First, you are obligated to take them home and then go where you wanted to go. This can become a major pain in the tail.

Secondly, there may come a time when you are very broke and are really going to need gas money to get back and forth to work until payday. If you haven't been insisting on gas money, it is very likely that they are not going to give you a penny. They will just find another way to work and not worry one bit about you. Trust me, it does happen that way.

It does not pay to milk the time clock. By that, I mean that you are taking more time to do the job than it normally requires, merely to increase your hours, and thus your paycheck. Bosses do not like that, and I can't really blame them for that. If you develop a reputation for doing that, it will severely handicap you when you ask for a raise.

In addition to that, when you run into problems doing a task that you were assigned, your boss will tend not to believe your explanation, and will figure that you were just goofing off again. This reputation will follow you from job to job and will make it harder to get another job in the first place.

Once in a while, you may run into a situation where you are working with someone that just got tossed into a job that they don't really know how to do. They know something about the job, but not enough to do it effectively. Unfortunately, someone called in sick or quit and there is no one more qualified available to do that job. The job absolutely has to be done, so they were stuck with it.

In that situation, please be very patient with that poor sod. Ignore their outbursts, they are just really frustrated at that point. Help them as much as you can, they can really use your help at that point. Remember, one of these days, that might just happen to you.

Sooner or later, you are going to be required to train someone on how to do your job. When this happens, please be patient with your trainee. Remember that you have been doing this job for a long time, while this is all new to them.

Another thing to remember is that everyone has their own way of doing things. You can show your trainee ways that work for you, and ways that work for other people; but they have to find the way that works for them. Even if their way seems totally awkward to you, if it gets the job done in the time allowed, leave them be.

When someone gets promoted from the working ranks to be a supervisor, it is expected that there will likely be one or two workers that cannot adjust to their management style and will quit rather than work for him. Please be patient with your new boss, it takes time to learn how to do a new job, especially that type of job.

Remember that he (or she) probably hasn't received any training in supervisory techniques. They are getting on-the-job training right now. The only employers that I know about that routinely give supervisory training are the military, not private sector employers.

A supervisor promoted from the ranks generally has the technical skills to do the job that you are doing. Now they are in the job of managing people and resources, though. It can be vastly more complicated, although it doesn't look like it.

Instead of depending on their own efforts to get the job done; they are now depending on a group of people to accomplish the tasks that they have been told to accomplish. Quite often, it seems that the tasks that they are told to do are impossible enough without the machines breaking down or dealing with contrary individuals.

To make matters worse, now they have to start dealing with paperwork and the bureaucracy of the company, much more than you or I have to deal with as individual workers. For example, what happens if one or more of their workers' paychecks get screwed up? First, that poor supervisor has to calm those people down and somehow persuade them to go back to work so that he can accomplish the tasks that he was set.

Then, he has to go through the system, find out exactly what went wrong, and then find out how to fix it. This all has to be done as swiftly as possible, so as to get his people's minds back on the job and not on their money that they haven't received. What is even worse is that he is just learning about the paperwork system. His people will not work worth a hoot until they know what has happened to their money and what is being done about it.

If this matter gets screwed up, he is liable to have a permanent morale problem. If that supervisor is working the second or third shifts, it gets even harder for him. It is a good possibility that he is going to have to come to the shop (during his time off!) when the payroll people are there so the problem can be fixed.

If you ever run into a supervisor that speaks ill of other workers in your presence, beware. They will do the same to you. This is one of the marks of the poorer type of supervisor. Stay away from that type as much as possible.

Occasionally, you may find yourself laid off from your job. If you know that it is going to be short-term and that you are going to be called back shortly, fine, then you can treat it as a vacation. If not, then allow yourself a short vacation (define its limits before you start it), and get busy finding a new job. Your unemployment compensation will not last forever. In any case, you never know how long that it will take you to find a new position.

Hunting a job is a full time job in itself. It is extremely easy to goof off on it. After all, no one is supervising you. You are just going to have to discipline yourself. If you don't, the end result is that you will either get a much poorer job or no job at all.

If you don't have a job, then sooner or later you are liable to end up living on the street. I can guarantee that you will not enjoy that.

It generally does not pay to work under the table. For starters, you are avoiding paying your fair share of taxes to support the government. You are risking getting in trouble with your government and that particular branch of any government tends to get very, very nasty about it.

Secondly, at least in the U.S., you are not accumulating any work credits to help with your retirement or disability claim. What happens if you get injured on the job? Your employer most likely will not pay for any medical bills that you incur.

You will also not be eligible for Worker's Compensation, as you would be on a regular job. You will not be eligible for unemployment if you are laid off. All in all, the money is nice, but you are taking a very high risk doing that sort of thing.

Not only that, you will not be able to put that job on your resume, so now you have a large gap of unemployment to explain to any possible future employers. To my mind, at least, all this trouble is not worth the hassle that you will go through.

If you ever get severely hurt on the job, where you have to draw Worker's Compensation, watch your behind! Especially if you are hospitalized and will need to draw it for some time, watch your behind! No matter how good a worker you are or how valuable you were to the company; you have just become a liability to the company.

You now represent a loss to the insurance company that your company uses. They are going to want to settle that loss as cheaply as possible. The insurance company may well put off paying you your weekly wage or medical bills, leaving you with no way to pay your ordinary bills, let alone your medical bills. How are you going to able to get to your doctor's or therapist's office, let alone paying them, with no money?

The insurance company may also hire people to spy on you to see if you are as severely injured as you claim to be. Make sure that you follow your doctor's restrictions on what you are able to do and what you cannot do! If the insurance companies catch you doing something that you aren't supposed to do, they are liable to claim that you are not as severely injured as you claim to be.

It doesn't matter that it was something that absolutely had to be done and you were the only person there that could do it (even at the cost of severe pain). It also doesn't matter that you were flat on your back, unable to move for two days afterwards. They have caught you doing something that you were supposed to be unable to do, therefore you are probably faking. This has a severe tendency to lower your settlement!

Make sure that you talk to an attorney, experienced in worker's comp. cases, before you sign anything. Follow his or her advice devoutly. Remember, they are experienced in this type of matters, you are not. You will also need to make sure that the settlement is going to cover the medical bills and expenses that you may start experiencing ten or twenty years down the road from this injury after you have accepted the settlement.

Always be polite to your customers, even if you dislike them. Remember, your company is in business to supply them with what they want and are willing to pay for. Those customers supply the money that your company uses to pay you.

If a customer comes in just when you are about to close, be polite and make sure that they get what they are looking for. Don't try to get them in and out of the store quickly, make sure that they are satisfied. They are not looking to cause you trouble; they are there to purchase a product or service that your business provides. Stay a bit later, at work, then normal if you have to, but make sure that your customer is satisfied.

Always be on your best behavior when your shop has a visitor. You want them to come away from their visit with a good impression of that business. Make sure that they do not get into trouble or hurt. You are aware of all the safety hazards there, and the ways to guard against them; your visitor may not be.

If you are employing or supervising someone; check up on their work occasionally, even if you trust them completely. People do change over the years and someone who is trustworthy doesn't always stay that way.

Still Working

My time is short;
I know it now.
Still, I'll stave
Off Death somehow.
My family needs
My love and care;
And still they need
Their daily fare.
The pain is now
Forever here.
But that is not
Why I fear.
What will happen
To those I love
When I can only
Give them love?
Tired, oh so tired,
Yet I carry on.
Far too soon,
My deathbed, I'll be on.
'Til that day
I'll do my best
To care for all their needs.
When I finally take my rest,
They'll know
I did my very best.

Wrongdoing

Caution

Caution pays
I swear, 'tis true;

Especially when
You're feeling blue.
When you're angry
Or distressed;
Your judgment, truly
Is not the best.
So when you are,
On the emotional scale,
Looking rather like
A whale;
Then take great care,
Be wary, be shy.
That way you'll not
Need an alibi.

If someone that is supposed to love and protect you abuses you instead; it does not mean that you are bad or that you deserved it. They are the ones doing wrong, not you. It is NOT your fault, really and truly.

Do not be afraid to apologize if you have done something wrong. It docs not show that you are weak, merely that you are human and not perfect.

Do not let your love for someone lead you into doing something that you know is wrong. Many a person has gotten into serious trouble that way.

If your friend asks you to do something that you know is wrong; tell them no and why. If they are truly your friend, they will respect your decision. They may get mad at you for the moment, but they will cool down and apologize later.

If you do not ever want to go to jail, then respect the rights of other people, especially when you are angry or desperate for money.

There may come a time when you are asked to take the blame for what someone else has done. Do not do it. They were willing to commit the crime, so let them suffer the penalty for committing it.

They will try very hard to convince you, but do not let yourself be talked into it. One argument that they will probably use is that you will not get into nearly as much trouble as they would. That is just to dangnab bad, they should have thought of that before they pulled their stunt.

You will get in enough trouble by yourself in your life, do not let someone talk you into taking the blame for what they did.

Never screw the little people. If you are bound and determined to steal, steal from institutions, not the poor guy who is barely making a living.

If you rip him off, you are also hurting the people who depend on him for support. I would much rather see you rob a bank than to mug someone. At least that way, you are not hurting the family that is depending on that person to make a living for them.

If you take 10,000 dollars from a bank, it will hurt the bank a lot less than it would hurt the person that you mugged and got fifty bucks from. That fifty bucks may be the difference between his kids eating that week or not.

There may be a time when you are charged with a crime you did not commit. Perhaps you are charged with something that you did do, but you feel that the circumstances justified your actions and the authorities disagree. My best advice to you is to tell the authorities to go fly a kite and proceed to trial. This is not necessarily the best legal advice, however.

The trouble with legal advice, though, is that your lawyer is not concerned with how you are going to live with yourself the rest of your life. He or she is merely concerned with the legal problem that they are hired for.

You are going to have to live with yourself and the results of your decision for the rest of your life. Your decision will be a lot easier to live with if you are certain that you did what you thought was right.

One day, you may be arrested as a result of your actions. I do not wish this to happen, no parent wishes to see his or her child in jail. It is a very hurtful thing to see someone that you love in jail or prison.

If you are released on bail, do not run away from the charges facing you. Humans have a life span of from sixty to seventy-odd years now. You are facing a maximum of how much time? Think this through before you start running. How much time will you have left on this planet after you have served your sentence?

If you start running away, you will always be looking over your shoulder for the authorities to catch you. Sooner or later, that tap on the shoulder will come, and you will not have enjoyed nearly as much the time that you have been free as you would have had you not been worrying about being caught. In addition to this, you will undoubtedly receive more time in jail or prison, than if you had just done your time in the first place.

Wouldn't it just be better to do the time and get it over with? Then you can get on with the rest of your life without worrying that you may be arrested at any moment for your past transgressions, and all that you have attained will be lost to you.

You are going to have to start all over once you are out of jail in any case. I assure you, it is better to start your life over once, rather than having to do it two or three times.

If someone has bailed you out of jail, they are trusting you not to run away. They are putting their money and/or property on the line for you. Do not betray their trust in you and flee your bail.

I know that it is very, very tempting to run away from the charges facing you. If you do that, however, you are only going to make matters worse in the long run. First off, you are screwing over the person who put up your bail. I assure you, screwing over someone who cares about you is always a bad thing to do.

Secondly, sooner or later, you are most likely going to get caught; and the judge will take a very dim view of your running away. It is almost certain that the sentence that he was considering giving you will be lengthened considerably.

You will have a whole lot more respect for yourself if you do not run away. If you feel like you are about to run, go to the nearest police station and turn yourself in. Tell them that you don't trust yourself not to flee bail anymore and so you are turning yourself in.

You will have a whole lot more respect for yourself and the authorities will tend to look at you a little more kindly. Now, mind you, you are

147

still going to have to suffer the punishment for whatever that you have done wrong, but you are on the road to changing your wrongful behavior.

If you do have to spend time in jail or prison, use that time constructively. Do not let it waste away like so many other people do. Think about why you are there in the first place and what you can do to prevent yourself from ever coming back to this place. Learn from your mistake. I assure you, if you have regard for the rights of others from now on, you will not be spending much time in jail.

While you are in jail, you may well be able to use that time to improve your education. Perhaps you cannot read or spell very well. Most jails have some kind of a library. Use it to improve your education or widen your field of knowledge. No knowledge is ever wasted.

Do not simply spend your time talking or playing games. You have only so much time on this planet, don't waste it.

Before you accuse someone of doing something wrong, be very certain of their guilt; especially in criminal cases. The "guilty beyond a reasonable doubt" standard is a good standard to use. If you are wrong, and they are innocent, you have severely harmed them and their reputation.

In most places there is a statute of limitations
for punishing someone who has done something
wrong. There is a reason for that. Think about it.

Prices

The jacuzzis
And the red silk sheets
Feel so nice;
But you had
Better look at
Their true price.
If your money
Comes from
Doing wrong;
Do you truly think
You'll have it
For long?

DAD

You've lain me over
Your bended knee.
Still later, I whined
Grounded, you see.
You clothed me
And sheltered me
All thru the years;
And you never let me

See you in tears.
For life was hard,
You worked a lot;
A family to feed
And you hurt a lot.
From dark 'til dawn
You worried at times;
And then you went
Back down to the mines.
The scars on your body
And the lines on your face
Tell the prices you paid
To give us a place.
So this is for you,
Our Father, so proud.
You, we could always
Pick out of a crowd.

The End

www.ingramcontent.com/pod-product-compliance
Lightning Source LLC
Chambersburg PA
CBHW051348280526
45784CB00007B/2870